No Frills, No Gloss,

Practical Cookbook

For Preparing Healthy Food

Bee photograph courtesy, Sebastien Rosset

Using Honey Instead of Sugar

If you use a sugar substitute, try 100% pure extract Stevia.

We support Diabetes Type One, Cancer Research & Motor Neuron Disease.
10% of the net sales will be divided equally between the charities.

DEVIL-FREE RECIPES WITHOUT ADDITIVES

Christine Thompson-Wells

Other books by Christine Thompson-Wells

Books for adults:

Making Cash Flow
39 Days & 39 Steps to Debt Recovery
How to Reduce Stress
Beat Stress in 20 Seconds
Stop Family Violence Now
Discover Your Selling Power
Selling Made Easy
How to Find Your Mind of Gold – Mind Power
The Game of Money & How to Play It
The Golden Book of Whispering Poems
How to Create Easy Flower Arrangements
How to Create Easy Wedding Bouquets
Healing & Wellbeing from Flowers & Plants

More adult books are written and will be released in the future

Audio books

Whispering Australian Native Flowers
Whispering Wildflowers
Whispering Roses
Whispering Lilies
Whispering Orchids
Devils In Our Food

Children's books

Will Jones Space Adventures & The Money Formula
Will Jones Space Adventures & The Money Formula – The Play
Will Jones Space Adventures & the Zadrilian Queen
Will Jones Space Adventures & The Children of the Black Sun
Seven more books in the Will Jones Series will be released.

PLEASE READ THIS INFORMATION

I have no financial or vested interested in any food company or food outlet. This recipe book has been written through my own collection of healthy food recipes. I have concerns for the lack of quality in the food products that we all buy. Through my extensive research with Devils In Our Food, it further raises the alarm bells as to what we are buying and feeding to our children and the family we love.

Food manufacturing companies need to be brought to account for the ingredients and additives they put into their manufactured food products. We now know many additives are making people ill and will become sick in the future. There will be more pain and heartbreak, higher medical bills, and more fatalities if food additives are allowed into food production and the growing techniques used in agriculture.

FOR YOUR INFORMATION

Respect for our food has been lost.

It is now time to have that respect put back into our life force.

For all people, respect for food is paramount for individual good health and wellbeing.

Food manufacturers have been dictating to the consumer, through bright and gimmicky advertising, to sell their products through visual appeal that does not always represent the quality and goodness of the product portrayed on its packaging image.

From the manufacturers, it is now time for honesty of the product and in the ingredients in the food we eat.

Prior to 2002, corporate food manufacturers could add up to 10 percent of food poisonous additives into their products.

From 2002, food manufacturers, are allowed to put 5 percent of poisonous food additive into their products.

A food manufacturer does not have to declare the poisonous food additives on the food information panel of the product if the additive is below 5 percent.

If a poisonous additive is 4.99 percent, you will not know if the food you are buying or eating has a food additive or multiple additives!

DEVILS IN OUR FOOD – LET'S CHANGE THIS SITUATION

For thousands of years we have grown or collected our food from healthy soil, rivers, and seas.

In the Twenty-First Century we are faced with polluted soils from fertilisers and contaminated seas and rivers. Our rivers and seas are polluted from the overuse and discarded plastics and fertiliser run off. Our marine life is under threat and our land environment is changing from global warming.

The nutritional value of the food we bought fifty – sixty years ago is no longer in the food we eat today. In many instances, we are paying good, hard-earned money for unhealthy food that will lead to illness in children and possibly premature death in many young people. We are in fact, eating ourselves to death.

For change to happen, we each individually need to take action for change to come about.

In my book, 'Devils In Our Food,' I've identified over 300 additives (devils) that are contributing worldwide to health problems in many people, including children. Long-term suffering from many diseases is on the increase and science, in many instances, is pointing to the food we are eating. Many foods, while growing in the fields, are sprayed with different fertilisers that are said to be safe, and years later, through illness, we find they are anything but safe. Once picked or harvested, such as corn, barley and other crops, these foods go through a series of processing where many food additive and preservatives are added.

If we look at dough mixes, including bread, a staple food not only eaten in Australia but worldwide, there are over sixty different poisonous additives that are used in different breads and cakes around the world.

In this new book on Devil Free Recipes – Recipes Without Additives, I'm introducing you to a new way of cooking and eating delicious food you can make at home.

The student is not forgotten, students on budgets can make mouth-watering food at the weekend or during holiday times, store it in the freezer and eat when needed.

I am sure some older folk would like to help busy working mums with preparing food. If the mums bought the ingredients and a copy of the recipe was given, many older people, if asked, would be happy to cook healthy food for their families and loved ones.

Let us enjoy the journey together and produce some exciting new recipes that can be eaten without fear.

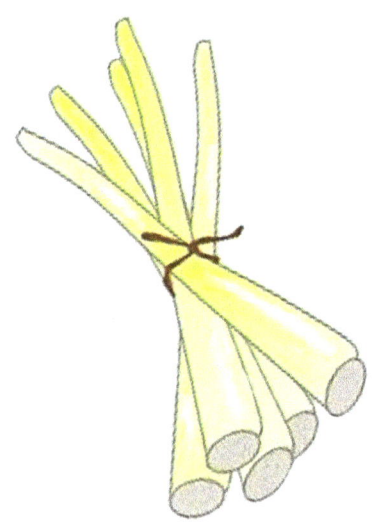

If you have purchased this book without its cover, it may be a stolen book.

Neither the publisher or the author is under any obligation to provide professional services in anyway, legal, health or in any form which is related to this book, its contents advice or otherwise.

The law and practices vary from country to country and state to state.

If legal or professional information is required, the purchaser, or the reader should seek the information privately and best suited to their particular needs, and circumstances.

The author and publisher specifically disclaim any liability that may be incurred from the information within this book.
All rights reserved. No part of this book, including the interior design, images, cover design, diagrams, or any intellectual property (IP), icons and photographs may be reproduced or transmitted in any form by any means (electronic, photocopying, recording or otherwise) without the prior permission of the publisher. ©

Copyright© 2020 MSI Australia

All rights reserved.

ISBN: 978-0-6481884-8-3

Published by Books For Reading On Line.com
Under licence from MSI Ltd, Australia
Company Registration No: 642923859
NSW, Australia

See our website: www.booksforreadingonline.com
Or contact by email: admin@booksforreadingonline.com
Covers and Copyright owned by MSI, Australia

MSI acknowledges the author and images, text and photographs used in this book.

www.how2books.com.au
booksforreadingonline.com

CONTENTS

	Page
Equipment you may need	1
Measurements	3
Organic, naturally grown or food you know the origins	6
Thickeners	7
Gelatin	7
Breakfast on the go	8
Breakfast	9
Great egg starters	
Crunchy bacon, cheese, spinach, and egg starters	10
Individual organic Italian cheese, turmeric, spinach and crunchy bacon muffins	12
Quiche with a difference – trout, avocado, Italian cheese, and tomato	14
Quick toasty treats – once made, can be kept in the fridge overnight and cooked the next morning	16
Egg and vegetable frittata – very Feta tasting	18
Egg, pork, and veal meat roll	20
Quick honey, vanilla, egg custard and blueberry topping	22
Quick lemon, egg custard with mandarin topping with organic honey or Stevia	24
Optional topping	26
Commercial cereal additives	27
Lunch	28
Vinegar and Gelatin	29
Healthy, Rainbow Light Salads	30
Beetroot, mint, carrot, and apple cider vinegar salad	31
Zingy, mango, apple cider vinegar mayonnaise	33
Amber tomatoes, corn, pepper, and apple cider vinegar salad	34
Green Granny Smith apple, amber tomatoes, and apple cider vinegar salad	36
Shades of blueberries and apple cider vinegar salad	38
Zesty Potato Salad	41
The story of flour	43
Using organic flour to make Fantastic Pies from 80 cents to $1.80 each!	44
Pie Pastry Recipe for Nine Pies - 90mm x 35mm pan	45
Pies make a satisfying meal and make packed lunches easy	47
Healthy energy giving pies	48
Pork and chicken pies	48
Pork and apple pies	50
Minced beef, onion, mushroom, red pepper and garlic pies	51
Sweet potato, potato, herb, and cheese sauce	53

Salmon or trout, potato, herb, and mornay sauce pies	55
Healthy food for hungry people	57
White fish and parsley sauce pies	58
More pies	60
Chicken and mushroom pies	61
Feta cheese and spinach pie	63
Beef and tomato pies	64
Feta, baby spinach, carrot, mushroom, and celery pie	66
Trans fats	68
Dinner	69
Chicken stock	70
Beef stock	71
Soups	72
Parsnip, lime, ginger, and organic coconut cream soup	72
Chickpea, coriander, and beef soup	73
Tomato and green basil soup	75
Celery, brown onion, and ginger soup	76
Cauliflower and organic Stilton cheese soup	77
Casseroles in a pan	79
Mushroom, beef, and red wine casserole in a pan	79
Chicken mushroom and white sauce – casserole in a pan	81
Lamb, parsnip, and red wine casserole in a pan	83
Fillet of beef, lamb, or goat – pastry-pocket roast	85
Tasty organic mushroom gravy – perfect with many meals	88
Goat, and red wine casserole with yogurt topping	89
Fresh salmon with lime sauce	92
Alternative side dishes – fried in organic olive oil. Vegetables – even children love them…!	93
Desserts	95
Quick chocolate, dark cherry, and pistachio custard	96
Fresh strawberry base, honey custard and raspberry topped slice	98
Cherry topped, honey, vanilla, gelatin, strawberry giant cupcake	100
Treats for children	103
Learning by doing – Quick healthy eating ideas for You and your family	104
Introducing Chrissy Cupcake	105
Basic honey, yogurt cupcakes	106
Butter, honey, and rosette cream topping cupcakes	108
Raspberry, jelly cupcakes	110
Chocolate cupcakes	112
FREE of honey and sugar blueberry cupcakes	114
Sugar-free blueberry jelly filling for cupcakes and other cake fillings	115
Happy times chocolate and strawberry large cupcake	118
Happy times large cupcake – strawberry topped cupcake	120
Introducing Saucy Sausage	121
Saucy skinless sausages for children's snacks, lunches, and parties	122
Tomato and cheeky beef sausages	122
Pork and apple cheeky sausages	124

Chicken, mushroom, parsley, and raspberry cheeky sausages with raspberry dipping sauce	125
Turkey, thyme, basil, and blueberry cheeky sausages with blueberry dipping sauce	126
Dipping sauce ideas	127
Mango dipping sauce	127
Mixed berries dipping sauce	127
Raspberry dipping sauce	128
Apple cider vinegar dipping sauce	128
Sausage for children's snacks, lunches and parties	129
Introducing Potato Pete and Sally Spud	130
Baked jacket potatoes – an exciting way to eat vegetables	131
Dora Damper would like to make your acquaintance…	132
Mini plain honey damper bread	133
Mini Raspberry topping damper bread	134
Mini Blueberry damper bread	136
Mini black currant, sultana, and honey damper bread	137
Mini date, fresh banana, cherry, and honey damper bread	138
Min organic very chocolate and pecan nut damper bread	139
Mini cheesy damper bread	141
Children's lunches from your kitchen	142
Biscuits	143
Cheesy straw biscuits – ideal for school lunches	143
Honey, ginger biscuits	144
Breads	145
Light, organic soda bread with yogurt and oats	146
Rye honey bread – rye bread with a difference	147
Tarts	149
Raspberry, honey and almond pastry fruit tarts with vanilla custard and fresh fruit topping	150
Honey, apple, and black currant tarts with meringue topping - the Meringue made without sugar	152
Raspberry, pecan flan with vanilla, creamed custard topping	155
Rose, lemon, and orange bundt cake	157

EQUIPMENT YOU MAY NEED

RECTRACTABLE, FLEXIBLE MEASURING CUPS OR MEASURING CUPS

2 LITRE MIXING BOWL

LINED BAKING TIN WITH GREASEPROOF PAPER

SELECTION OF UTENSILS

MORE UTENSILS YOU MAY NEED

OTHER UTENSILS

LARGE AND SMALL COOKING POTS

LARGE AND SMALLSOLID FRYING PAN – PREFERABLY WITH LIDS

MOULDS FOR GELATIN-BASED FOODS CAN BE OF MANY DIFFERENT SHAPES AND SIZES

MOULDS ARE A HANDY ACCESSORY IN THE KITCHEN. THEY CAN BE EXPENSIVE BUT ONCE BOUGHT, CAN LAST A LIFETIME TIME

SERVING PLATES – A SELECTION OF DIFFERENT SERVING DISHES MAKE ALL THE DIFFERENCE TO YOUR EFFORTS

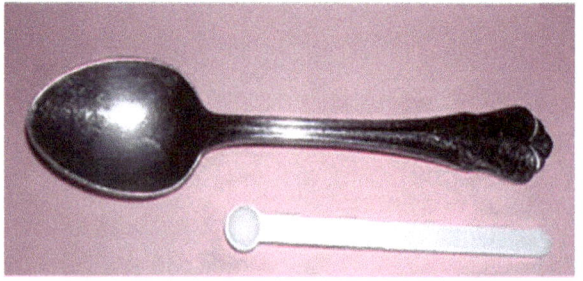

DIFFERENT SIZE SPOONS TEASPOON AND WHITE NATURAL STEVIA SWEETNER SPOON

Measurements

Teaspoon, Tablespoon, Dessertspoons, Cups, Quarts and Gallons

1) 1 teaspoon (tsp or t)
2) 2 teaspoons = 1 dessertspoon (dstspn)
3) 3 teaspoons = 1 tablespoon
4) 4 Tablespoons = 1/4 cup
5) 5 Tablespoons + 1 teaspoon = 1/3 cup
6) 8 Tablespoons = 1/2 cup
7) 1 cup = 1/2 pint
8) 2 cups = 1 pint
9) 4 cups (2 pints) = 1 quart
10) 4 quarts = 1 gallon

Volume Conversion

1) 1 Tablespoon = 3 teaspoons = 15 millilitres
2) 4 Tablespoons = 1/4 cup = 60 millilitres
3) 1 ounce = 2 tablespoons = 30 millilitres
4) 1 cup = 8 oz. = 250 millilitres
5) 1 pint = 2 cups = 500 millilitres
6) 1 quart = 4 cups = 950 millilitres
7) 1 quart = 2 pints = 950 millilitres
8) 1 gallon = 4 quarts = 3800 millilitres = 3.8 litres

US Liquid Cups to Metric

1) 1/4 cup = 60 mL
2) 1/3 cup = 70 mL
3) 1/2 cup = 125 mL
4) 2/3 cup = 150 mL
5) 3/4 cup = 175 mL
6) 1 cup = 250 mL
7) 1 1/2 cups = 375 mL
8) 2 cups = 500 mL
9) 4 cups = 1 litre

Volume: Metric to Imperial

1) 25 ml. equals 1 fl oz
2) 50 ml. equals 2 fl oz
3) 75 ml. equals 2 1/2 fl oz

4) 100 ml. equals 3 1/2 fl oz
5) 125 ml. equals 4 fl oz
6) 150 ml. equals 5 fl oz
7) 175 ml. equals 6 fl oz
8) 200 ml. equals 7 fl oz
9) 225 ml. equals 8 fl oz
10) 250 ml. equals 9 fl oz
11) 300 ml. equals 10 fl oz
12) 350 ml. equals 12 fl oz
13) 400 ml. equals 14 fl oz
14) 425 ml. equals 15 fl oz
15) 450 ml. equals 16 fl oz
16) 500 ml. equals 18 fl oz
17) 600 ml. equals 1 pint
18) 700 ml. equals 1 1/4 pints
19) 850 ml. equals 1 1/2 pints
20) 1 litre equals 1 3/4 pints
21) 1.5 litres equals 2 3/4 pints
22) 2 litres equals 3 1/2 pints
23) 2.5 litres equals 4 1/2 pints
24) 3 litres equals 5 1/4 pints[1]

Weight by Spoon and Other Measures

1) 1 teaspoon = (t) or (tsp)
2) 1 gram = (g)
3) 1 litre = (L)
4) 1 cup of flour is equal to 120 grams (g)
5) 3 cups = (360g)
6) 1½ tsp = (7ml)
7) 1 cup butter = (240g) butter
8) 1½ cup sugar (300g)
9) 1 Tbsp = (15ml) dried herbs
10) 1 cup = 225g sour cream or yogurt
11) 2 Tbsp = (30ml) finely chopped vegetables or lemon, lime or orange peel
12) 3 Tbsp = (45ml) honey, treacle, golden syrup, or treacle
13) 1 Tbsp = (15ml) fresh lemon, lime, fruit juice
14) 1 dessertspoon (dstspn) = (30g)

---

[1] https://www.thespruceeats.com/recipe-conversions-486768

Other Liquid Measures

Cup	Metric	Imperial
¼ cup	63ml	2¼fl oz
½ cup	125ml	4½fl oz
¾ cup	188ml	6⅔fl oz
1 cup	250ml	8¾fl oz
1¾ cup	438ml	15½fl oz
2 cups	500ml	17½fl oz
4 cups	1 litre	35fl oz

Oven Temperatures

Celsius	Fahrenheit	Gas Mark
120	250	1
150	300	2
160	320	3
180	350	4
190	375	5
200	400	6
220	430	7
230	450	8
250	480	9

Organic, Naturally Grown or Food You Know the Origins

I have continually used the word 'Organic' throughout this book but if you know the origins of the food and produce you are buying or using, and you feel comfortable this is what you want to eat, then please use these recipes accordingly.

Organic means, foods that are from the natural environment. It also means there are no forms of additives, fertiliser, growth hormones, growth regulators, pesticides, herbicides, or synthetic chemicals used in the growing production, or production of the produce. The word Organic also identifies that the plant or plant materials are not genetically modified (GMO) or contain modified organisms.

With such a standard in place, it means that the consumer, when buying, can be assured that the standards or origins of the product are healthy and good to eat.

Christine

THICKENERS

Organic corn flour needs to be a product of 100 percent certified organic.

Organic arrowroot is a starch useful as a thickener in custards and desserts, sauces, soups and in baking; it can also be used as a replacement, when honey is added, as a replacement for icing sugar. Extracted from the Maranta Arundinacea plant it is also good for the human digestive and immune system.

Organic tapioca flour is also a starch and a popular ingredient used in wheat-free recipes. It can be used to thicken soups, pie fillings, gravy, and sauces.

Organic potato starch has a smooth texture and can be used instead of wheat flour or corn starch; is also used as a thickener.

Please note

If you are using thickeners in your recipe, make the flour or starch into a paste before adding it to the wet cooking ingredients. By doing this, while stirring, the thickener blends evenly with the ingredients and does not allow clogging or lumping. When a thickener is added to the recipe, always continue stirring until the ingredients and thickener blend together as one when cooked.

Gelatin

When adding gelatin to any recipe, buy pure, unflavoured 225 bloom gelatin. This is a high-grade product.

Grass fed organic, beef gelatin is the best gelatin to buy.

Gelatin cannot be obtained from any plant-based source. It is obtained from grass fed beef. Gelatin provides eight of the nine essential amino acids not synthesized by the human body but are essential to maintain good health. Gelatin promotes gut and digestive health, helps to maintain, and stabilise appetite which assists with healthy eating habits and reduces food craving. It also helps with establishing weight control, assists with muscle recovery after exercise or injury; helps to develop strong bones, reduce pain and inflammation in joints; assists with hair and nail revitalisation and assists in developing a healthy immune system.

BREAKFAST ON THE GO…

A different approach to breakfast is needed. Packaged cereals, for the most part, give you unsustainable energy, add weight to unwanted places and most of all, they are of little to no food value to your important body and brain.

When you feel light-headed half way through the morning, you will know that your sugar levels have dropped; you don't have the energy to do another job and the meeting or job to be done by a certain time seems almost impossible to do! This is the sign of eating energy lacking, processed or over processed food. The food has been robbed of its health benefits, possibly has a number of poisonous food additives added, which if under 5%, do not have to be listed on the food packaging or ingredient panel, and frankly, it is not worth the package it's been packaged in.

Breakfast has been underrated for many decades. In many countries around the world, if passing fast food takeaway, junk food outlets, the queues of people in their cars or work trucks waiting to be served and waiting for their breakfast order is bewildering. Young males from the age of 20 – 45 years, studies have shown, are the most vulnerable people caught up and are within this unhealthy habit of eating. Like all of us, we can each develop such habits. Sadly, it is not until a little later in life, that the illness attached to bad eating habits shows itself in ill health.

Breakfast is by far the most important meal of the day. Leaving home without *breaking the fast*, for that is what breakfast does, is doing yourself a great injustice. To think I will get a coffee and muffin on the way to the office or work will do you no good in the long term…!

Most manufactured muffins have a variety of additives in their ingredients. Now more widely used than at any other time in our flour or dough making history is the additive 920 L-cysteine monohydrochloride. This additive is linked to a number of different illnesses, including, 'brain and nervous system damage,'.[2] It is also linked to cancer.

The breakfast recipe ideas that follow will give you some great ways to make healthy changes to such an important meal of the day.

---

[2] http://www.fao.org

Breakfast

There are many breakfast combinations that can be made using eggs; breakfast does not have to be boring and uninviting.

Following I have used ingredients that could be seen as not edible in such a recipe book, the main one being bacon or ham. The bacon to avoid is bacon with added nitrites. Commercially used nitrites are developed by extensive heating which creates nitrosamide which is highly dangerous and is used in many preserved meats.

GREAT EGG STARTERS

Crunchy bacon, cheese, spinach, and egg starters

These little starters are light and easy to make.

Ingredients - pastry

130g plain, organic flour
¼t non-aluminium baking powder
¼t ground organic rock or Himalayan salt
Organic freshly ground pepper to taste
⅓ cup organic olive oil
Water to moisten

Ingredients – Filling

6 large organic eggs
35g organic Feta cheese
25g finely chopped yellow or red pepper
25g finely chopped organic spring onion
35g finely chopped organic spinach
35g finely chopped organic ham or bacon
¼t Himalayan or rock salt and organic freshly ground pepper to taste.

Method - pastry

- Cut unbleached baking paper into 6 x 6inch squares (15cm x 15cm) Add a little olive oil to each tray cup to secure paper when placed in the tin.
- Combine flour, oil, salt, pepper, and baking powder in a mixing bowl and with your finger tips rub through so that all ingredients blend. Add water (a little at a time. (Make a soft dough). Roll out pastry. Cut into 6 even squares (same size as paper). Place into paper cups

Filling

- Beat eggs until blended
- Add all cut ingredients
- Stir together
- Pour into pastry cases

Preparation Time 20 minutes

Cooking Time 45 minutes or until golden brown

Oven Heat 180°

Tip: Many flours contain additives that the human body cannot process. Buy flours that are well labelled. If doubtful, ask the producer what is in the flour? Some flour contains additive 220, sulphur dioxide, a bleaching agent which can lead to serious health conditions or illness.

Cut unbleached baking paper

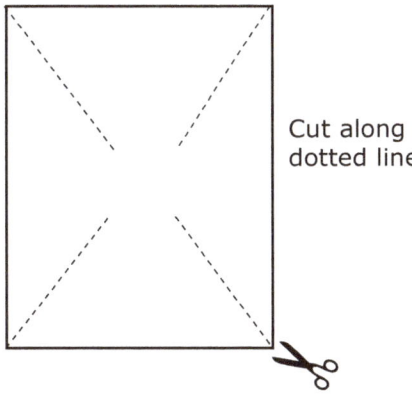

Cut along dotted line

Paper lining shapes:
Tear from roll a 6inch (15cm x15cm) piece of baking paper, fold in two, cut along fold line then follow the directions opposite.

Place cut paper into baking previously oiled tray cups. By lightly oiling the tray cups it allows the paper to stick securely while adding the ingredients.

Work flour, oil, salt, pepper, and baking powder mixture evenly through fingertips until blended. Then add sufficient water to make a soft dough ball. Cut dough into 6 equal square shapes.

Beat eggs, add remaining ingredients while folding all ingredients.

Raw ingredients added to the uncooked pastry cases ready for baking.

These little gems can be cooked the night before and warmed ready for breakfast the following morning.

Individual organic Italian cheese, turmeric, spinach, and crunchy bacon muffins

Not only great for breakfast but great to take on picnics or to the beach...

Ingredients

6 large organic eggs
100g plain organic flour
60g Grana Padano flaked cheese
¼t non-aluminium baking powder
Ground Himalayan or rock salt to taste
Pepper to taste
2 small finely chopped mushrooms
35g finely chopped shallots
2 sprigs finely chopped fresh parsley
1 sprig finely chopped fresh thyme
20g finely chopped fresh baby spinach
60g organic cooked bacon
½t organic turmeric
⅓ cup organic olive oil.

Method

- If muffin paper cases are not greaseproof, coat with olive oil
- Cook bacon until its crispy, put to one side
- Beat eggs until yolk and white are evenly combined
- Slowly add flour then add all remaining ingredients
- Bake and enjoy

Preparation Time 20 minutes

Cooking Time 45 minutes or until golden brown

Oven Heat 180°

Tip: Grana Padano cheese has no additives or artificial colours. Many cheeses have added food additives, this gives them flavour and texture appeal. Additive 102, Tartrazine is one of many additives used to colour different cheeses and other foods; additive 102 is highly poisonous.

Bacon cooking until golden brown.

Combined ingredients in muffin cases ready for baking.

Cooked, golden delicious muffins ready to eat.

These foods can be cooked at the weekend, stored in the fridge, and eaten through the week.

A protein and veggie packed breakfast to keep you going until lunch time.

Quiche with a difference – trout, avocado, Italian cheese, and tomato

Sometimes we need to give ourselves a treat – if you like trout, this may be just what you need; it is also great to have for a delicious family treat.

Ingredients - pastry

200g plain organic flour
¼t non-aluminium baking powder
¼ cup organic olive oil
½t Himalayan or rock salt
½t organic pepper
½ - ¾ cup water

Ingredients – Filling

6 large organic eggs
½ ripe avocado
75g small organic cut tomatoes
Ground Himalayan or rock salt to taste
Pepper to taste
120g fresh trout cut into small sections
1 cup freshly chopped parsley
25g Grana Padano flaked cheese
½ cup organic full cream milk

Topping

125 g organic small and cut tomatoes.

Method – pastry

- Grease quiche dish with olive oil
- Blend together the flour, baking powder, salt, and pepper
- Add the olive oil to flour mixture
- Slowly add water to form soft dough – do not add too much water, roll out and,
- Line dish with pastry

Filling

- Beat eggs
- Add all ingredients and milk to mixture
- Slowly stir together – keep fish in flakes (do not beat)
- Pour into pastry case
- Add extra tomatoes for topping

Preparation Time 30 minutes

Cooking Time 1 hour or until golden brown.

Oven Heat 180°

Tip

Other fresh or sustainably caught tin fish can be used in this recipe.

Work flour, oil, salt, pepper, and baking powder mixture evenly through fingertips until blended. Then add sufficient water to make a soft dough ball. Line olive oil greased container with pastry.

Prepare all vegetables ready for mixing.

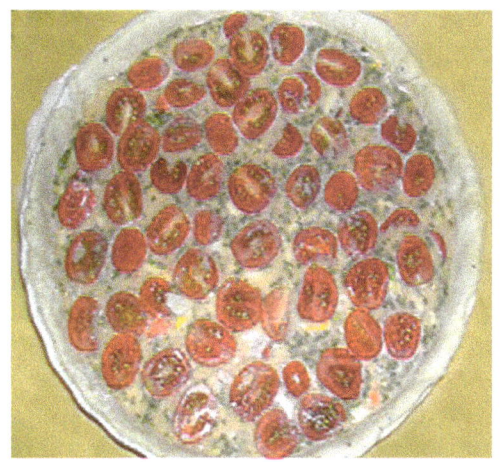
Freshly made quiche ready for baking.

Freshly baked and ready to eat...

Quick toasty treats – once made, can be kept in the fridge overnight and cooked the next morning

Sometimes, we just need a quick and easy breakfast or have something ready for that early morning start…! This recipe can be prepared the night before.

Ingredients –

6 slices organic rye bread
6 medium to large organic eggs
1 medium thinly sliced tomato
½ cup fresh organic baby spinach
2 rashers (non-sulphite) bacon sliced in strips
5g finely chopped baby spinach
35g goats cheese
35g organic Feta cheese
35g organic Brie cheese
½ cup organic freshly chopped parsley and chives
Organic olive oil
Himalayan salt to taste
Freshly ground pepper to taste to taste.

Method

- Heat oven 220 degrees
- In a pan, cook bacon over hot fast heat until crunchy
- Cut greaseproof paper as shown on page 11, and place in baking tray cups
- Cut crust off bread
- Sprinkle olive oil over bread (not too much, enough to moisten)
- Roll bread with a rolling pin. This will loosen the bread fibres and allow it to bend into the muffin tin shape
- Line the baking cups with the rolled bread.

Filling

- Place 1 round of finely cut tomato into the base of the bread
- Choose one of the cheeses and gently combine cheese and 1 tbsp of parsley and chive. (35g of cheese will serve 2 portions)
- Spoon evenly into 2 of the bread lined cups in the baking tin
- Sprinkle with cut baby spinach
- Once muffin cups are full of ingredients, crack a single egg for each muffin cup
- Continue this method for the remaining 4 muffin cups.

Preparation Time 30 minutes.

Cooking Time 15 minutes.

Oven heat 220°

Tip: A light, energy giving sustainable breakfast that will keep you going for hours.

Fresh organic rye bread.

Cut crust from the bread. Doing this allows the bread to become pliable and easy to use.

Place a cut slice of bread into each muffin cup.

Add a thinly sliced tomato portion to each muffin cup.

Add the desired cheese filling, top with spinach or parsley.

Top with a freshly cracked egg.

Cook in a hot oven (220 degrees for 15 minutes or until eggs are cooked.

Serve with a crunchy bacon topping and freshly toasted organic or homemade rye bread toast.

Egg and vegetable frittata – very Feta tasting…

Ingredients

6 organic large eggs
75g organic, finely chopped, red cabbage
75g organic, finely chopped white cabbage
75g organic, chopped baby spinach
75g organic, finely cut fresh carrots
25g organic, finely cut red, yellow or green pepper
2 large organic shallots or ½ organic, finely chopped red onion
200g organic cubed feta cheese
¼ cup organic olive oil.

Topping

75g Grana Padano flaked cheese.

Method

- Grease container (20 x 13cm container or similar size) with a little extra olive oil
- Whisk eggs until well mixed
- Add all cut vegetables, olive oil to egg mix
- Put all ingredients into greased container pushing down hard to release any air pockets
- Evenly disperse flaked cheese topping.

Preparation Time 20 minutes

Cooking Time 45 minutes or until golden brown.

Oven heat 180°

Tip: If vegetables are soft, always crisp up before using them as an ingredient. To do this: fill the sink with very cold water, submerge all ingredients and leave to drink in the moisture for 2 or more hours. Thirsty vegetables and salad foods all benefit from this technique.

Chopped and mixed vegetables, including olive oil.

Once the vegetables are mixed, carefully add cubed Feta cheese.

Ingredients placed into greased baking container. To give a solid pie, makes sure all air is removed from mixture before baking.

Add flaked cheese for the topping.

Bake until golden brown.

Serve with fresh salad or freshly baked organic jacket potatoes.

Egg, pork, and veal meat roll

A protein packed breakfast roll that can last the week. This is not only great for breakfast but also lunch or dinner.

Ingredients

750g pork and veal organic mince meat
7 large organic eggs (5 to boil, 1 for glazing or topping and 1 for binding meat mince and ingredients)
1 dstspn organic dried Italian herbs
½ cup organic wholemeal flour
Himalayan salt to taste
Organic black pepper to taste

Topping

Beaten egg used for glazing.

Ingredients ready to combine. Flour to be added once egg, mince, shallots, and herbs are combined.

Method

- Boil 5 eggs for 4 minutes, run under water to cool, shell eggs
- Finely cut shallots
- Put meat mince into a large bowl
- Sprinkle Italian dried herbs over mixture
- Add flour
- Break egg over mixture and hand combine to mix all ingredients
- Combine thoroughly until the mixture is firm
- Once combined, place on floured BPA-free cling film
- With flattened mixture, place the five remaining eggs in a row, roll mixture over eggs
- To secure meat and eggs, lift the meat roll and tightly roll again in cling film
- Release cling film
- Place on baking paper sheet on baking tin
- Coat with the beaten egg
- Bake until ready.

Oven Heat 180°

Preparation Time 30 minutes.

Cooking Time About 1 hour or until golden brown

Tip: This full of nutrition egg roll is ideal for children and adult lunches.

All ingredients are combined and placed on floured cling film.

Cooked eggs, in a row, on the mince mixture.

Roll in cling film to make secure shape.

Unroll shape onto greased paper and glazed meat with beaten egg.

Bake until golden brown and allow to cool before cutting.

Once cut, this energy giving meat roll can be served with salads, toast, and other delicious toppings.

Quick honey, vanilla, egg custard and blueberry topping

Because of the egg content, an ideal treat anytime; this recipe also makes an energy-sustainable breakfast.

Ingredients

6 large organic eggs
1½ L full cream organic milk
1 dstspn pure vanilla extract
3 dstspn organic corn flour (or organic arrowroot or tapioca)
3 dstspn organic honey
2½ dstspn pure gelatin (not synthetic)
Please see the information on page 7 for gelatin

Topping

400g organic (thawed) frozen or fresh berries
1½ dstspn pure gelatin
2 dstspn organic honey. (12 servings)

Method

- Line tin with BPA-free cling film
- In a mixer or hand blender, blend the eggs until whites and yolks are completely blended, once blended, slowly add vanilla and honey
- (With a little of the milk combine the gelatin, cornflour, arrowroot, or tapioca, make into a paste before adding to the eggs and vanilla.)
- Slowly warm the remainder of the milk on the stove, when warmed
- Slowly stir all ingredients together
- Gently, continue to stir until all ingredients are thoroughly mixed
- Continuously stir until mixture thickens. Do not hurry the cooking time.

When the mixture has thickened, pour into a lined cling filmed tin, and allow to thoroughly cool or place in the refrigerator.

Preparation Time: 20 minutes

Cooling-time About 3 hours or overnight.

Topping Slowly warm, in a saucepan on the stove or in a bowl in the microwave, the berries, gelatin, water and honey. Do not boil or overcook, spread evenly over the top of the custard and allow to cool, preferably overnight.

Tip: Pure gelatin is good for growing bones, skin, gut and bowel health and helps with the human digestive system.

Line a 23cm x 23cm (9") tin with cling film. Make sure the film fits easily into the corners of the tin.

Recently seen on BBC television within a science and medical program were a series of experiments on food prepared in a microwave. The outcome of the trials revealed no ill-effects were incurred and the quality and integrity of the food was maintained.

Gently fold the eggs making sure both yolks and whites are well blended.

The custard mixture slowly cooking on the stove; continuous stirring is essential.

When thickened, remove from heat, and spoon into cling-lined container. The custard needs to be cold before adding the blueberry topping.

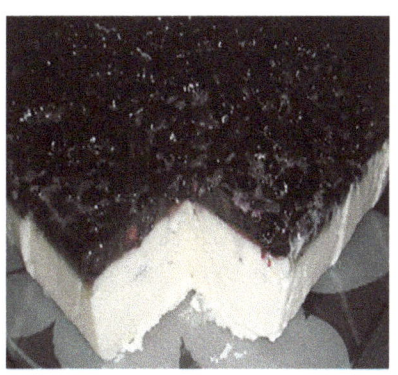
A great recipe and treat that can serve 12 people; it can be made well in advance or kept in the fridge for after school treats.

A delicious breakfast treat, full of good nutritional and natural ingredients that will help to keep your body healthy and your mind sharp.

As you go through the custard recipes within the book, I speak of different ways to make a custard; you may develop your own preferred way.

Quick lemon, egg custard with mandarin topping with organic honey or Stevia

Ingredients

6 large organic eggs
1½ L full cream organic milk
1 dstspn pure vanilla extract
4 dstspn organic arrowroot
3 dstspn organic honey (or substitute with (optional 4 spoons of pure organic Stevia, please see page 2 for spoon measurements)
2½ dstspn pure gelatin.

Topping

6 fresh mandarins
2 fresh lemons
1½ dstspn pure gelatin
2 dstspn organic honey or substitute with pure organic Stevia
¼ cup of water or pure organic fruit juice if required.

(12 servings)

Method

- Line a 23cm x 23cm (9") tin with cling BPA-free cling film. Make sure the film fits easily into the corners of the tin.
- In a mixer or hand blender, blend the eggs until whites and yolks are mixed; once mixed, slowly add vanilla and honey
- (With a little of the milk combine the gelatin, cornflour, arrowroot, or tapioca, make into a paste before adding to the eggs and vanilla.)
- Slowly warm the remainder of the milk on the stove, when warmed
- Slowly stir all ingredients together
- Gently, continue to stir until all ingredients are thoroughly mixed
- Continuously stir until mixture thickens. Do not hurry the cooking time.

When the mixture has thickened, pour into lined cling filmed tin, and allow to thoroughly cool or place in the refrigerator

Preparation Time 20 minutes

Cooling Time About 3 hours or overnight

Allow to stand and cool

Topping Peel and remove any white fibre from the mandarin segments, keep segments separate. Cut lemons in half and squeeze to extract juice. Once the custard is cooled, place mandarin segments in a pattern on the custard.

Slowly warm in a saucepan on the stove the gelatin, lemon and fruit juice and honey. Do not boil, allow to cool for 1 minute. Drizzle gelatin, lemon, and honey mixture over mandarins.

Blend the egg whites and yolks together. Once blended, add the other ingredients.

Tip The gelatin and honey base will help the mandarins retain their moisture.

Pour blended mixture into a pan, continuously stirring. Do not stop stirring until mixture has thickened.

Once thickened, remove from heat, and spoon into the cling- lined container.

Once cooled, about 3 hours, add a fruit topping.

Decorate custard with your chosen fruit topping.

Cut into 12 equal portions. A zesty starter for any breakfast treat – it will keep your taste buds zinging...!

Optional topping

Once you have a firm base of egg custard, the topping for this delicious breakfast starter is unlimited.

Custard topped with fresh mandarins, raspberry, and blueberries. Once in place drizzle with dissolved honey, gelatin organic fruit syrup.

Cut into squares, this custard makes a delicious mouth-watering breakfast.

Commercial cereal additives

Please check all commercial processed cereals before buying the 'food in a box'. Some of the additives below are used in children's cereals, baby food and baby formula. This a frightening list which covers, synthetic, artificial food colours, flavour enhancers, bleaching agents, synthetic antioxidants, petroleum-based food additives, some of which are used in phosphate fertilizers. Some food additives add to the supermarket shelf life of products while other additives are used as a food volume increaser therefore adds to weight gain. Other food additives may be by solvent extraction, methanol, and petroleum. Some additives are combined with phosphates.

Code	Name	Type
102	Tartrazine	Food colour
150c	Caramel III	Flavour enhancer
110	Sunset yellow FCF	Food colour
150b	Caramel II	Flavour enhancer
223	Metabisulphate	
270	Lactic acid	Maybe synthetic
303	Potassium ascorbate	
315	Erythorbic acid	
320	Butylated hydroxyanisole (BHA)	
321	Butylated hydroxytoluene	
338	Phosphoric acid	
339	Sodium phosphates	
341	Calcium phosphates	
359	Ammonium adipates	
381	Ferric ammonium citrate	
412	Guar gum	
416	Karaya gum	
445	Glycerol esters of rosin	
452	Potassium polymetaphosphate	
463	Hydroxypropyl cellulose	
482	Calcium lactylate	
511	Magnesium chloride	
519	Copper II	
540	Dicalcium diphosphate	
576	Sodium gluconate	
951	Aspartame, Nutrasweet, Equal	
966	Lactitole	

Please remember: if a product has less than 5% of food additive, it does not have to be listed on the ingredient panel of the product. For a complete and comprehensive identity of food additives, please see my book: Devils In Our Food at www.booksforreadingonline.com

LUNCH

Vinegar and Gelatin

Vinegar

Vinegar has been used for thousands of years and there is a reason we've had this in our diets. Accordingly, and more recently, *'vinegar has been found to help reduce weight and visceral (abdominal) fat, improve lipids and insulin sensitivity'*. A study has also revealed that adding vinegar daily to a diet will reduce post-meal sugar demands. Vinegar has been shown to reduce appetite, delay food breakdown into sugars in the gut, and add to gut wellbeing.

Organic apple cider vinegar is unfiltered, naturally fermented and contains mother enzymes. It also contains natural acetic acid, gallic acid, and catechin; these properties are antimicrobial, antidiabetic and help in lowering cholesterol and lowering high blood pressure.

My mother once told me, *'your grandmother drank two diluted dessert spoons of apple cider vinegar in water daily'*. She had beautiful skin and always looked exceptionally well.

Gelatin

Pure gelatin is a natural source of protein from grass fed beef cattle; it is pure protein which contains up to natural 18 amino acids. Amino acid cannot be made by the body; the body needs its supply from the food you eat. When protein is consumed in our diets, the protein in the intestinal tract is broken down into individual amino acids; once processed by the gut, the amino acids are reconstructed into new amino acids, this process is called protein biosynthesis.

Amino acids are described as a pool and consist of about 120 – 130gm in an adult male, less in females. The main objective of the amino acid pool is to be complete and preserved. If one or more of the amino acids in the pool are missing or not sufficient, the production of protein is weakened, and the body's metabolism function is limited. The body's signs are indicated through weight problems, hair loss, sleep disorders, skin problems, arthritis, cardiovascular imbalance, diabetes, mood swings, high cholesterol, menopausal problems, and high blood pressure.

Healthy, Rainbow Light Salads

Beetroot, mint, carrot, and apple cider vinegar salad

You will need a 750ml container for this recipe.

Ingredients

400g cooked, organic beetroot
Sprigs of mint, parsley, and chives (not too much, enough to add flavour)
800g shredded organic carrot
1 small organic finely cut shredded red pepper
5g finely cut shredded shallot, leek or red onion
¾ cup organic apple cider vinegar
Light squeeze of lemon
Himalayan salt or natural rock salt
Organic pepper to taste
2½ dstspn gelatin
½ cup (off the boil) hot water to add to the gelatin
Organic olive oil to grease the mould.

Method

- Lightly grease the inside of the container with olive oil
- Wash and dry all ingredients
- Cut finely: beetroot, mint, parsley, chives, carrot, shallot (or red onion) and red pepper
- Put all cut ingredients in the bowl add the lemon juice, Himalayan salt and freshly ground pepper
- Mix, by hand, thoroughly through; try not to bruise the vegetables
- Once mixed through, add the mixture of gelatin, apple cider vinegar, and off the boil water. Please see the instructions below for gelatin
- Put ingredients into the mould gently pushing down with your hand
- Make sure the ingredients fit into every part of the mould releasing any trapped air.

Gelatin Grass fed beef gelatin is the best gelatin to buy. In a separate bowl, add, off the boil, water to the gelatin while continually stirring. The mixture of gelatin and water need to be completely clear with a slight lemon colour. Once dissolved, stir the Apple Cider vinegar into the gelatin mix. Keep stirring until all ingredients are well mixed. Add to the vegetable mix. Once in the mould, gently tap on the bench to settle ingredients.

Preparation Time 20 minutes

Cooling Time About 3 hours. Overnight cooling is recommended.

Tip Apple cider vinegar acts as a healthy food preservative.

Olive oil greased mould.

Cooked organic beetroot finely chopped.

Carrot and herbs added to the beetroot.

Gelatin-based vegetable mixture in the mould ready to be cooled.

When cool and solid, up end the mould onto a serving dish. Firm, delicious beetroot salad ready to serve.

A refreshing different salad and an ideal side salad with fish or meat.

This red salad can be served with boiled eggs, a different combination of foods and zingy mango, apple cider mayonnaise.

Zingy, mango, apple cider vinegar mayonnaise

Ingredients

100g organic fresh or thawed frozen mango
1 large free range or organic egg
½ cup whole fat, organic fresh milk
½ cup organic apple cider vinegar
1t organic arrowroot
Light squeeze of lemon
Freshly ground black pepper
Himalayan or organic rock salt to taste, not too much.

Method

- Pulp mango until the fibres are broken, this can be done with a kitchen whiz
- Strain the pulped mango through a sieve until juice is extracted, discard solid remains
- In a separate bowl, beat the egg until well blended
- Blend about a tablespoonful of the milk with the arrowroot to make a fine paste
- Put the remains of the milk in a saucepan and allow to slowly warm on the stove, do not boil
- When hot, while stirring, add the arrowroot mixture to the milk, continue stirring while adding the mango, lemon juice, beaten egg, apple cider vinegar, pepper, and salt - do not boil
- Once thickened, remove from the heat, and pour into a serving jug.

Preparation Time 20 minutes

Cooling Time About 30 minutes

Tip: This sauce is a great companion for many dishes including light egg salads, fish meals and as a dipping sauce.

Eggs are a nutritional meal at any time

Amber tomatoes, corn, pepper, and apple cider vinegar salad

You will need a 750ml container for this recipe.

Ingredients

Organic olive oil to grease the mould
340g organic yellow tomatoes (halved)
40g small organic yellow peppers finely chopped
10g organic shallot or leek finely chopped
90g organic cooked corn kernels
Rind zest of 1 medium orange
Squeeze of lemon
½ cup apple cider vinegar
Himalayan or organic rock salt to taste
Freshly ground organic pepper to taste
2½ dstspn gelatin
½ cup (off the boil) hot water to add to the gelatin.

Lightly grease the mould with olive oil.

Cut the tomatoes into halves.

Method

- Lightly grease the inside of the container with olive oil
- Wash and dry all ingredients
- Cut finely pepper, shallots, or leeks, cut kernels from corn cob
- Grate the rind from one orange
- Combine all cut ingredients in a bowl
- With all ingredients in the bowl add the lemon juice, Himalayan salt, and freshly ground pepper
- Mix, by hand, thoroughly through - try not to bruise the vegetables
- Once mixed through, add the gelatin mixture of apple cider vinegar, and off the boil water
- Put ingredients into the mould gently pushing down with your hand
- Make sure the ingredients fit into every part of the mould.

Gelatin: Grass fed beef gelatin is the best gelatin to buy. In a separate bowl, add, off the boil, water to the gelatin while continually stirring. The mixture of gelatin and water need to be completely clear with a slight lemon colour. Once dissolved, stir the Apple Cider vinegar into the gelatin mix. Keep stirring until all ingredients are well mixed. Add to the vegetable mix. Once in the mould, gently tap on the bench to settle ingredients.

Preparation Time: 20 minutes

Cooling Time: About 3 hours. Overnight cooling is recommended.

Tip: Some studies have suggested that vinegar can increase feelings of fullness and help you eat fewer calories.

   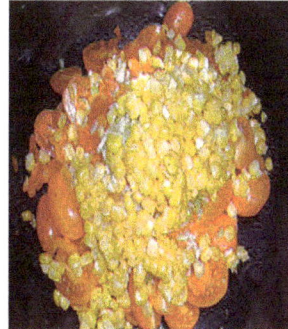

Add cut tomato halves and pepper.	Add finely cut shallot or leek.	Cut, with a sharp knife, the kernels from the cob.	Add to vegetables.

Zest of the orange tops this golden glow of vegetables.

Gently combine, including the salt and pepper, into the dry ingredients.

The gelatin, and vinegar mixture is added to the dry ingredients.

 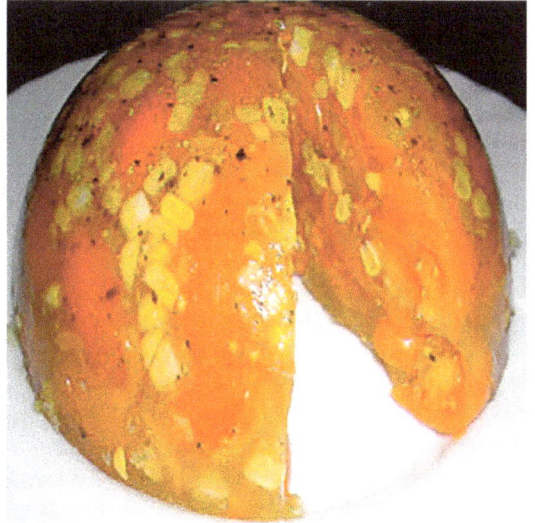

When set, up-end the mould contents onto a serving dish.
This sparkle of colour is firm, delicious and ready to serve.

Refreshing and zesty – is great with most summer foods.

Green Granny Smith apple, amber tomatoes, and apple cider vinegar salad

You will need a 750ml container for this recipe.

Ingredients

100g cut and organic finely shredded white cabbage
50g finely cut and shredded organic baby spinach
Sprig of parsley finely chopped
½ large green organic apple (with skin on) finely chopped.
5g finely shredded or finely cut organic shallot or leek
15g small yellow organic pepper, finely cut and shredded
1 brown organic mushroom finely cut
Light squeeze of lemon
¾ cup organic apple cider vinegar
Himalayan salt or organic rock salt to taste
Organic ground fresh pepper to taste
2½ dstspn gelatin
½ cup (off the boil) hot water to add to the gelatin
Organic olive oil to grease the mould

Topping: 8 small tomatoes cut in halves to cover the base.

The mould oiled with olive oil

Method

- Lightly grease the inside of the container with olive oil
- Wash and dry all ingredients
- Cut finely: cabbage, baby spinach, parsley, apple, shallot (or leek) and yellow pepper
- With the ingredients in the bowl add the lemon juice, salt and freshly ground pepper. Mix, by hand, thoroughly through; try not to bruise the vegetables
- Once mixed through, add the gelatin mixture of apple cider vinegar and off the boil water
- Put ingredients into the mould, gently pushing down with your hand. Make sure the ingredients fit into every part of the mould.

Gelatin Grass fed beef gelatin is the best gelatin to buy. In a separate bowl, add, off the boil, water to the gelatin while continually stirring. The mixture of gelatin and water need to be completely clear with a slight lemon colour. Once dissolved, stir the Apple Cider vinegar into the gelatin mix. Keep stirring until all ingredients are well mixed. Add to the vegetable mix. Once in the mould, gently tap on the bench to settle ingredients.

Topping: Decorate the base with halved tomatoes

Preparation Time: 20 minutes

Cooling Time: About 3 hours. Overnight cooling is recommended.

Tip: Can accompany many meat, fish or egg dishes.

Shredded cabbage.

Apple and spinach added to the cabbage.

Shredded pepper added to the ingredients.

Added chopped mushroom – all ingredients are kept small this adds to the delicacy of the flavour.

The base is decorated with bright amber, organic tomatoes.

Once set, the salad can be upended onto a serving dish.

A colourful, savoury salad ready to serve.

Shades of blueberries and apple cider vinegar salad

You will need a 750ml container for this recipe.

Ingredients

150g thinly cut, organic baby purple carrots
225g organic blueberries
200g frozen organic blueberries
50g thinly cut, organic red cabbage
5g thinly cut, organic shallots
Himalayan salt or rock salt to taste
Freshly ground organic pepper to taste
Light squeeze of lemon
¾ cup organic apple cider vinegar
2½ dstspn gelatin
½ cup (off the boil) hot water to add to the gelatin
Organic olive oil to grease the mould.

Thinly cut organic red cabbage.

Method

- Lightly grease the inside of the container with olive oil
- Wash and dry all ingredients
- Cut finely carrots, cabbage, and shallot
- Leave blueberries whole
- With all the ingredients in the bowl add the lemon juice, salt, and freshly ground pepper. Mix, by hand, thoroughly through; try not to bruise the ingredients
- Once mixed through, add the gelatin mixture of apple cider vinegar and off the boil water
- Put ingredients into the mould, gently pushing down with your hand. Make sure the ingredients fit into every part of the container.

Gelatin: Grass fed beef gelatin is the best gelatin to buy. In a separate bowl, add, off the boil, water to the gelatin while continually stirring. The mixture of gelatin and water need to be completely clear with a slight lemon colour. Once dissolved, stir the apple cider vinegar into the gelatin mix. Keep stirring until all ingredients are well mixed. Add to the mixture. Once in the mould, gently tap on the bench to settle ingredients.

Preparation Time: 20 minutes

Cooling Time: About 3 hours. Overnight cooling is recommended.

Tip: The least handling of vegetables the better. If your vegetables seem soft prior to using, re-cut stems, soak in very cold water overnight – they will be perfect for preparation the following day.

Ingredients, gelatin and apple cider vinegar added and allowed to set.

The set salad ready for serving.

Like all the salads mentioned in this section, blueberry salad can be served with a range of meat or fish dishes. These salads are perfect for family gatherings, celebrating national days, holiday season or a casual lunch.

Keep all gelatin-based foods cool until ready to serve.

Red beetroot salad.

Amber tomato salad.

Green cabbage and Granny Smith apple.

Shades of blueberry salad.

Zesty Potato Salad

Ingredients

500g organic, skin on, finely chopped potatoes
1 large organic, skin on, finely chopped, Granny Smith apple
1 finely cut organic shallot
5g parsley
5 leaves, organic, finely chopped mint (2 leaves for adding to the cooking potatoes)
1 sprig finely chopped organic thyme
or
½ t organic dried thyme
¼ cup organic olive oil
Squeeze of lemon to taste
¼ cup organic apple cider vinegar
½ cup organic yogurt
1 beaten organic egg yolk
Himalayan or rock salt to taste
Organic pepper to taste

Dressing: 1-2 thinly sliced organic oranges.

With mint, gently cooking potato pieces.

Method

- Wash all ingredients
- Cut potato into small cube or square shapes
- Cook until firm, not hard (do not over boil or cook)
- When cooked, run under cold water, pat dry, and add to a mixing bowl
- Cut apple into small or square shapes, add to bowl
- Cut shallot into fine, see through pieces, add to bowl
- Chop parsley and mint into fine pieces, add to the bowl of ingredients
- Add olive oil, yogurt, lemon, beaten egg yolk, salt and pepper to ingredients
- With a fork, slowly mix the ingredients (do not break or mash the ingredients)
- Make sure the wet mixture of egg, olive oil, yogurt and lemon juice are well mixed through the potatoes and apple pieces

Dressing: Decorate with orange halves.

Preparation Time: 20 minutes

Cooling Time: About 30 minutes

Tip: To stop the apple from browning while preparing other ingredients, squeeze lemon juice over the cut fruit, then cover with a damp tea towel or paper towel.

For good sized potato and apple pieces, 3 pieces of apple or potato should fit onto 1 teaspoon.

Cooked potato and apple added together.

Shallot, parsley, mint, and thyme added to the ingredients.

Gently mix through the firm ingredients, then add the yogurt, vinegar, lemon juice, beaten egg and olive oil.

A refreshing, light potato and apple salad can be served with many meat or fish dishes. This can be made a day or two prior to any event or family meal.
Tip: once made, cover with a damp cloth or paper towel, this will stop browning or drying of the ingredients.

The Story of Flour

Unadulterated flour has been used by thousands of generations over thousands of years. Unfortunately, in today's world, flours used in many of the world's bread, cake, sweet and savoury dough food is not represented by the flour our ancestors used.

Many of the flour products eaten by millions of people worldwide have dangerous food additives. Out of over 100 dough additives, I have mentioned just a few below. Extracted from my book: Devils In Our Food.

Humectants – keeps food moist and allows for a longer shelf life in cakes, bread, rolls, and other baked foods bought at the bakery, supermarket, and other food outlets.

120 Cochineal or carmines or carmic acid. Can cause allergies, hyper-sensitive reactions, asthma, gastrointestinal disorders, skin ailments, eczema, dermatitis, itching and hives.

142 Green S. Causes asthma, urticaria (inflamed reddened patches on the skin), depression, anger, difficulty in sleeping, difficulty in concentrating, especially in children.

170 Calcium carbonate also calcium carbonate (i) and (ii). High doses may contribute to mineral imbalances in the human body. Can also contribute to confused behaviour, haemorrhoids, kidney stones, abdominal pain, constipation, anal bleeding, and fissures.

200 Sorbic acid. Is linked to hyperactivity and behavioural problems. Can cause skin conditions: eczema, dermatitis, itching and hives. Is linked to cancer and liver damage.

213 Calcium benzoate. Is linked to: *'...birth defects increased significantly in combination with aspirin, brain damage, neurological disorders, cell mutations, testicular cancer, chronic urticaria, dermatitis and delayed growth.'*[3] Not recommended for consumption by children.

221 Sodium sulphite, sulfite. May cause severe reactions in asthmatics, cause headaches, migraine, intestinal upset, skin disorders and ailments, eczema, and dermatitis; creates behavioural problems, can contribute to ADHD, cause gastric irritation and nausea.

---

[3] http://thearticlebay.com

Using Organic Flour, Make Fantastic Pies from 80 cents to $1.80 each!

Pie Pastry Recipe for Nine Pies - 90mm x 35mm pan

PASTRY

Ingredients

100g (1 cup) organic self-raising, flour
100g (1 cup) organic plain flour
¼ cup organic olive oil
¼ tsp of Himalayan or rock salt
¼ tsp ground black pepper
¼ cup of water
1 whipped organic egg for topping
¼ cup of organic milk for topping

Tips
Heat the oven to 180 degrees before placing pies in the oven.

This dough quantity makes either 6 large pies or 12 small pies

Roll out the dough ball to 2ml thickness.

Dough ball ready for cutting into three.

Dough ball cut into three.

Tip
Do not overwork the pastry otherwise the dough will become tough this is due to overworked gluten.

Method

- Put both flours into a large mixing bowl and blend together
- Add salt, pepper, and olive oil
- Blend the ingredients together with your fingertips; they should resemble fine breadcrumbs
- When all ingredients feel evenly mixed, slowly add the water.
- Work the dough into a ball
- Cut, the dough ball into 1/3 sections (by cutting the dough ball this way, 2/3rds are kept for the pie shells and 1/3rd for the pie tops)
- Grease each individual pie compartment of the pie tin with olive oil or line with paper
- With a pastry cutter, cut the pastry to the correct size to line the bases of the pie tin
- Once cut, insert the cut pastry into position in the tin
- Add your chosen pie ingredients. Please see the collection of pie filling on the following pages
- Once the pie filling is in the pastry shell, brush the exposed edges of the shells with the egg and milk mixture
- With the 1/3 section of dough remaining, cut smaller circles to fit neatly on the pie top.
- Once in place, brush with the egg and milk mixture, then squeeze the top and bottom of the case together forming a tight top and bottom
- Pinch pie edges together. Snip the pie top with scissors. During baking, this allows some of the steam to escape and stops the pie from exploding.

Oven Heat 180°

Cooking Time: about 45 minutes or until the pastry is golden brown.

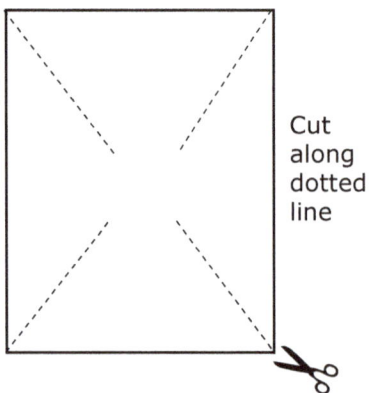

Cut along dotted line

If you choose to use baking paper, follow the directions above.

Once the paper is cut, put into baking tin. I sometimes put a small drop of oil in the tin before adding the paper, this keeps the paper in place.

Empty pie cases cut (2ml thick) ready for filling.

Filled pie cases with the pie tops attached and brushed with egg and milk, once baked, this forms a golden topping.

A cooked pie ready to eat.

Pies make a satisfying meal and make packed lunches easy

Salmon and potato pies

Below: Pork and apple pies

Below: White Fish and Parsley Sauce pie

Opposite: Feta Cheese and Spinach pie

HEALTHY, ENERGY GIVING, PIES

Pork and chicken pies

Ideal for student, work lunches or a family picnic. For savoury pies use the pastry recipe on page 45.

Ingredients

200g organic pork mince
200g organic chicken mince
½ Tsp organic Italian herbs
1 small organic shallot for base flavour
Himalayan or organic rock salt to taste
Organic, freshly ground pepper to taste
1 dstspn organic olive oil.

Topping

1 beaten organic egg
¼ cup of organic milk for topping.

Stock

1 cup homemade chicken stock, please see page 70
1 dstspn of organic gelatine.
Himalayan salt and organic pepper to taste.

Time

Bake for 45 minutes or until golden brown.

Oven Heat 180°

Tip

Homemade pies can be frozen, so making batches when you have time adds to their great benefits. Healthy pies to go with summer salads, for work, school, or university lunches. Or easily warmed through on a winter's night.

Method

- Most butchers will mince meat. If not using mince, cut the meat into small cubes
- Gently heat the olive oil in a pan (keep the heat low do not burn the oil)
- Add cut shallot, Italian herbs (do not overcook)
- Add the cut meat or minced meat
- Slowly cook for about 10 minutes (do not overcook)
- Remove, and allow to cool
- Spoon meat into pastry cases
- Brush pie edges with egg and milk topping mix
- Add about 1 dstspn of stock to each pie filling
- Secure pie top, brush with egg and milk topping mix
- Insert a large opening in the top of the pie (this allows the steam to escape and later, to inject the gelatin and chicken thickener)
- Bake in the oven. Allow to cool, once cooled insert with a funnel and insert gelatine and chicken stock into pie opening. Leave to cool and for the gelatin to set.

Gelatin mixture

After baking the pies, in a small saucepan, gently warm chicken stock, once warm, stirring constantly, slowly add the gelatine; once combined insert the mixture, via a funnel, into cool pies. Allow to cool in the refrigerator.

Tip Serve cold.

Pork and apple pies

For savoury pies please use the pastry recipe on page 45

Pie filling ingredients

2 small, peeled Granny Smith apples
375g organic pork mince
1 small shallot finely chopped
1 Tsp organic Italian herbs
1 cup chicken stock (please see page 70)
1 dstspn organic gelatin
2 dstspn organic olive oil
Himalayan or organic rock salt to taste
Organic, freshly ground pepper

Topping

1 beaten organic egg and
¼ cup of organic milk for topping

Time

Bake for about 45 minutes or until crisp and golden

Oven Heat 180°

Tips

The apple inside filling should be drier rather than wet

If the pie centre seems dry after baking, make a small opening in the lid, warm ½ cup of chicken stock, add a teaspoonful of gelatin and mix until clear. Through a funnel insert the liquid into the pie and allow to cool before serving.

Cold pork and apple pie make a great lunch when served with summer salads.

Method

- Make pastry as described on page 45
- Create the pastry case shells ready for the meat and apple filling
- Peel and core the apples
- Cook in a saucepan with a little water until soft, mash with a fork or vegetable masher, leave to stand
- Cook shallot in heating olive oil in a separate pan
- Add to the pan, the pork mince and Italian herbs, cook for about 5 minutes
- Remove from the pan and add to bowl
- Warm chicken stock (please see page 70), add gelatin to warmed stock
- Add stock and gelatin mixture to pork and mix
- Spoon into empty pastry cases (leave enough room for a teaspoonful of apple)
- Once pies have their filling, brush pastry sides with egg and milk topping, top with a pastry lid, brush with egg and milk topping
- Cook in a pre-heated oven 180°.

Minced beef, onion, mushroom, red pepper and garlic pies

For savoury pies please use the pastry recipe on page 45

Pie filling ingredients

350g minced organic beef
2 small red peppers sliced
1 small clove organic garlic
2 organic sliced mushrooms
1 small organic sliced red onion
1 cup water for gravy
1 dstspn organic olive oil
Himalayan or organic rock salt to taste
Freshly ground pepper to taste.

Thickener

½ cup of water
1 dstspn organic self-raising, flour or organic arrowroot for thickening.

Topping

1 beaten organic egg and
¼ cup of organic milk for topping.

Time

Bake for about 45 minutes or until crisp and golden.

Oven Heat 180°

Tip

Extra pepper, while cooking in the oven, marinates within the beef and gives you a warm glow inside when eating the pie.

Method

- Make pastry as described on page 45
- Create the pastry case shells ready for the meat filling
- Heat the oil in a pan
- Cook onion, pepper and garlic until golden brown or caramelized
- Add meat and mushrooms to the cooking pepper, onion and garlic
- Allow all ingredients to cook through for about 5 minutes
- Add one cup of water to the mixture and allow to warm. (If you feel the mixture is too dry, slowly add more water until a medium dense gravy has formed)
- In a small bowl or cup, mix the flour (arrowroot) with ½ cup of water to form a paste
- Stirring the meat mixture and gravy add the flour (arrowroot) mixture to the cooking ingredients
- Once thickened, take from the heat and spoon into the waiting pastry cases
- Brush pastry cases with egg and milk topping
- Top with the pastry lid and brush with the egg and milk topping mixture
- Cook in a pre-heated oven 180°.

Healthy homemade pies are good to eat any time of the year...!

Sweet potato, potato, herb, and cheese sauce

For savoury pies please use the pastry recipe on page 45

Ingredients

2 dstspn organic olive oil
100g diced organic pumpkin
100g diced organic sweet potato
3 medium organic diced or cubed mushrooms
10g thinly cut leek, onion, or shallots
1 Tsp organic Italian dried herbs
Himalayan or organic rock salt to taste
Organic, freshly ground pepper to taste

Pie cheese sauce

Freshly chopped or organic parsley
1½ cups full cream organic milk for sauce
50g Grana Padano hard cheese or similar
2 dsrtpn organic self-raising, flour (or organic arrowroot thickener)
¼ cup milk for flour to make paste thickener

Topping

1 beaten organic egg and
¼ cup of organic milk for topping.

Time

Bake for about 45 minutes or until crisp and golden.

Oven Heat 180°

Tip

The baked vegetables should appear with baked edges that are crisp and darkened; this adds to the baked vegetable flavours of the pie.

Method

- Make pastry as described on page 45
- Create the pastry case shells ready for the vegetable and cheese sauce filling
- Clean, dice all vegetables into small manageable pieces
- Add all vegetable to a large pan ready for oven baking
- Cover with olive oil and brush to make sure all vegetables are covered
- Sprinkle salt and pepper to taste over vegetables
- Bake in a hot oven (220) until golden brown. Some vegetables, because of their water content, may take longer to cook
- As the vegetables brown in the oven, in a saucepan add the milk to warm for the pie sauce
- Add the parsley to warming milk
- Add the cheese to the warming milk and parsley, stir
- In a separate container, make a paste with the flour or arrowroot and ¼ cup of milk
- As the milk and cheese warms, slowly add the paste to the warming milk
- Continue to stir until the sauce thickens
- When cooked, remove vegetables from the oven and put into bowl ready to add the cheese sauce
- Once sauce is thickened add the sauce to baked vegetables and fold to make the mixture
- Fill the pastry case with the vegetable and cheese sauce mixture
- Brush pastry case edge with milk and egg
- Top the pastry case with the pastry lid and brush with the egg and milk topping.

Serve with fresh vegetables or a green salad.

Raw vegetables prior to baking.

Baked vegetables ready to be added to the cooked cheese sauce mixture.

Cheese and parsley sauce ready to be added to the baked vegetables.

Healthy, nutritional pies are a great standby food. Any combination of fillings can be used, even leftovers from a Sunday roast. Why not experiment and ask the family what type of filling they would like in your latest pie creation...?

Salmon or trout, potato, herb, and mornay sauce pies

For savoury pies use the pastry recipe on page 45

Ingredients

100g or 2 small portions of fresh salmon or trout
5g finely cut organic leek
2 sprigs of organic parsley
2 medium, finely diced, organic potatoes
1 dstspn organic olive oil
Himalayan or organic rock salt to taste
Organic, ground pepper to taste.

Mixed herb sauce

1 dsrtsp organic self-raising, flour or organic arrowroot for thickening
1½ cup whole cream organic milk
¼ cup milk for thickening
¼ Tsp of parsley, oregano, lemon thyme, thyme, and coriander
75g hard cheese (Grana Padano or similar)

Topping

¼ cup milk
1 beaten organic egg

Time

Bake for about 45 minutes or until crisp and golden.

Oven Heat 180°

Tip

Serve hot with fresh or deep-fried vegetables.

Method

- Make pastry as described on page 45
- If still attached, remove the skin from the fish
- Cut fish into small, diced portions
- Simmer oil in the pan, allow to heat
- Add leek and parsley allow to cook through
- Add fish, try to keep the fish in whole pieces
- Gently cook for about 5 minutes
- Remove the fish from the pan and allow to stand while the sauce is made
- In a saucepan, gently bring to boil, the finely diced potatoes in the water
- Once boiled, remove from the heat, drain, and allow to stand

Sauce

- After removing the fish, pour the remaining milk into the warm pan containing the herbs
- Allow to warm
- Mix ¼ cup milk with the flour or arrowroot to form a paste, keep stirring the mixture
- Add to warming milk and cooked herbs, keep stirring, then
- Add the cheese to the warming milk
- Once thickened, spoon the sauce into the bottom of the pastry case
- Add the cooked fish and potato
- Cover with the remaining sauce
- Brush pastry case edge with milk and egg
- Top the pastry case with the pastry lid and brush with the egg and milk topping mixture
- Cook in a pre-heated oven 180°

Serve with your favourite vegetables or healthy salad.

The fish is cooked keeping it in whole pieces.

Empty shells of pie cases have the sauce then the cooked fish added.

If you have sauce leftover, keep it to drizzle over the pie and vegetables once they are served.

Healthy food for hungry people

White fish and parsley sauce pies

For savoury pies use the pastry recipe on page 45

Ingredients

100g white, deep sea caught, fish (cut into equal small chunks, not too small)
5g organic red onion, leek, or shallots
5g fresh finely chopped parsley
1 finely medium, diced organic potato
1 dstspn organic olive oil
Himalayan or organic rock salt to taste
Organic, freshly ground pepper to taste

Parsley sauce

1 cup whole cream organic milk
¼ - ½ milk for thickening
1 dsrtsp organic self-raising, flour or organic arrowroot for thickening
5g fresh, finely chopped parsley
Himalayan or organic rock salt to taste
Freshly ground organic pepper to taste

Topping

1 beaten organic egg and
¼ cup of organic milk for topping.

Time

Bake for about 45 minutes or until crisp and golden.

Oven Heat 180°

Tip

Serve fish pies hot and, if any left over, drizzle with white parsley sauce to add to the flavours.

Serve with a variety of deep-fried vegetables. Please see page 94

Method

- Make pastry as described on page 45
- Add oil to heating pan and let warm
- Add onion, leek or shallot and let brown
- Add white fish chunks and diced potato
- Allow to cook through (about 5 minutes)
- Gently move ingredients in the pan while cooking

Sauce

- Pour 1 cup of milk into the pan to warm
- Mix ½ milk with the remaining parsley, flour, or arrowroot to form a paste
- Add to warming milk, keep stirring
- Once thickened remover from the heat
- Spoon the sauce into the bottom of the pastry case
- Add the cooked fish and potato to the sauce in the pie base
- Cover the fish and potato with the remaining sauce
- Brush pastry edge with milk topping
- Top the pastry case with the pastry lid and brush with the egg and milk topping mixture
- Cook in a pre-heated oven 180°

Serve with your favourite vegetables.

Tip

If you feel the potatoes are a little too firm after removing the fish, leave in the pan to cook a little longer, then remove and add to the fish.

Serve pies with deep-fried vegetables for something different. Please see page 94

MORE PIES

All growing and developing children and young adults need to eat substantially healthy food. The young brain of young adult does not fully mature until the person is in their mid-twenties. From birth, both the body and brain need to be well nourished. The age-old pie is a power-packed food that can be made over a weekend, if a student, through holiday or semester breaks and at other home times.

The pies shown in this section cost between 80cents to $1.80 each to make. For as little, or less, as $9.00, these are 6 nutritious meals. This makes the humble pie an affordable alternative. By comparison – 'junk food,' which can cost significantly more, does not give the nourishment a homemade pie can offer.

Once the pastry is made, the inside ingredients are only limited by your imagination.

Making our own food can have significant health benefits: kneading a piece of dough, pounding a piece of steak into submission can reduce stress. Reducing stress is good for the brain as endorphins are released, stress is then lessened in the body and your wellbeing is supported by the food you are eating.

Cooking and the preparation of your food can become a part of your own philosophy of life, when this happens, our children see the reflection and differences in their own lives. Not only that, by watching and taking part in creating their food, allows a child to develop their own life skills, which they will take into their own adult lives.

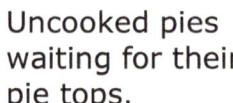
Uncooked pies waiting for their pie tops.

Chicken & Mushroom pies

For savoury pies use the pastry recipe on page 45

Ingredients

1 dstspn organic olive oil
200g free-range, diced organic breast of chicken
3 organic diced mushrooms
5g red onion, leek. or shallots
2½g freshly chopped parsley
½ Tsp organic Italian herbs
Himalayan or organic rock salt to taste
Freshly ground organic pepper to taste
½ cup organic self-raising, flour or organic arrowroot for flouring the chicken
1 cup whole cream organic milk

Chicken sauce

½ cup homemade chicken stock. Please see page 70
¼ milk for thickening
1 dsrtsp organic self-raising, flour or organic arrowroot for thickening
2½g fresh, finely chopped parsley

Topping

½ cup whole cream organic milk
1 beaten organic egg

Time Bake for about 45 minutes or until crisp and golden

Oven Heat 180°

Tip

Serve hot or cold, ideal for younger and older student lunches, working lunches. Keep in the freezer for future lunches – a meal that is so affordable.

Method

- Make pastry cases as outlined on page 45
- Heat oil in a pan
- Add the onion, leek or shallots, parsley and allow to brown do not overcook)
- Add fresh parsley
- Put the flour into a bag, together with Italian herbs, mix or shake
- Add the chicken to the flour and herb mixture
- Shake to cover the chicken pieces
- Add the flour covered chicken to the cooking parsley and leek
- Add the mushrooms
- Brown the chicken and mushrooms, keep turning both, do not leave to cook too long as the chicken will go stringy and loose its delicate flavour
- Once all pieces of chicken show a delicate browning add the sauce

Chicken sauce

- Mix the stock, milk, thickening and parsley into a paste.
- Slowly, while stirring, add the paste to the cooking chicken and milk. Do not stop stirring. Stir until the chicken and sauce are well mixed
- Once the mixture has thickened, spoon into the empty pie shells
- Brush pastry edge with milk and egg topping mixture
- Top the pastry case with the pastry lid and brush with the egg and milk topping mixture
- Cook in a pre-heated oven 180°

Serve with a salad or warm vegetables.

Pastry cases ready for the chicken and mushroom filling.

Cooking shallots and fresh parsley.

Flour ready to cover the chicken.

While gently stirring, the milk is added to the cooking ingredients.

Pies, ready to eat...

Best served hot with steaming freshly cooked vegetables.

Feta cheese and spinach pie

For savoury pies use the pastry recipe on page 45

Ingredients

10g shallots
180g diced organic feta cheese
100g chopped organic baby spinach
2 medium organic eggs to combine the mixture
Himalayan or rock salt to taste
Freshly ground organic pepper to taste

Topping

1 whipped organic egg and
¼ cup of organic milk for topping

Time Bake for about 45 minutes or until crisp and golden

Oven Heat 180°

Tip When in season, buy spinach, rinse well, cut or chop into generous portions, lightly steam, strain off cooking water, bag, or container the spinach and freeze for use at a later date.

Method

- Make pastry cases as outlined on page 45
- Soak and clean the spinach if needed
- Cut or chop spinach
- Cut the feta cheese into chunks
- Thinly slice the shallots
- Add the above ingredients to a mixing bowl
- Beat the eggs until well blended
- Add the eggs to the spinach mixture, mix well until all ingredients are covered by the egg mixture
- Add the mixture to the pastry cases
- Top the pastry case with the pastry lid and brush with the egg and milk topping mixture
- Cook in a pre-heated oven 180°

Serve with a salad or warm vegetables.

Beef and tomato pie

For savoury pies use the pastry recipe on page 45
A beefy pie for winter comfort...

Ingredients

500g organic minced beef
1 dstspn organic olive oil
1 medium sliced organic red onion
1 chopped organic clove garlic
1 Tsp organic Italian herbs
½ tin organic tomatoes
Himalayan or organic rock salt to taste
Organic, freshly ground pepper to taste

Topping

1 beaten organic egg
¼ cup of organic milk for topping

Beef sauce

½ cup beef stock, please see page 71
2 dstspn organic flour or arrowroot for thickening
¼ cup water for thickening.

Time Bake for about 45 minutes or until crisp and golden.

Oven Heat 180°

Tip The tin tomatoes add a depth and rich flavour to these pies; your family will love them.

Method

- Make pastry cases as outlined on page 45
- Heat oil in a pan
- Add the sliced onion and garlic
- Add the salt and pepper, allow all ingredients to cook until transparent
- Once cooked add the meat, making sure the meat mince is separated as it cooks with the other ingredients, allow to brown
- Once browned, add the tinned tomatoes, and allow to cook for about 10 minutes
- Once the ingredients are cooked through, in a separate bowl, mix the beef stock, flour and ¼ cup of water to make a paste
- Slowly add the paste to the cooking meat. At this point, if the mixture is too dry, slowly add a little extra stock
- Once mixed add the cooked meat mixture to the pastry cases
- Brush pastry edge with milk and egg topping mixture
- Top the pastry case with the pastry lid and brush with the egg and milk topping mixture
- Cook in a pre-heated oven 180°.

Serve with a salad or deep-fried vegetables, please see page 94?

Please note: Homemade pies are a rich form of complex carbohydrate which helps the brain to function and the body to have both the carbohydrate to do a day's learning or a day's work. Together with the carbohydrate is the protein of the filling which allows both the body and brain to work effectively. Pies are an energy giving food. Like all foods, pies should be eaten in moderation.

Pastry cases ready for their pie filling

Uncooked pie cases waiting for their pastry tops

A tasty pie just waiting to be eaten...

Feta, baby spinach, carrot, and mushroom pie

Ingredients

Organic olive oil for greasing the dish
100g organic finely chopped or grated red cabbage
50g organic, finely chopped or grated green cabbage
25g organic, finely chopped or grated baby spinach
100g organic, finely chopped or grated carrots
100g organic, finely chopped red or gold pepper
20g organic finely chopped or grated red pepper
2 organic finely chopped shallots
½ organic finely chopped or grated red onion
250g organic feta cheese
6 free range eggs
Himalayan salt to taste
Organic, ground black pepper to taste

Topping

75g hard cheese (Grana Padano or similar) for topping the pie

Time

Bake for about 50 minutes or until crisp and golden.

Oven Heat 180°

Tip

This is a good standby for busy parents. Do not freeze.

Method

Use 200 by 130ml container

- Prepare all vegetables. If you have washed them, make sure they are dry before using
- Grease the dish with olive oil
- By hand, mix the vegetables together
- Beat the eggs, add the cheese, and mix by hand
- Hand fill the pie dish pushing the ingredients firmly into the corners and into the dish
- Sprinkle or top with Grana Padano or similar cheese.

Grease the container with oil prior to adding the pie mixture.

The pie complete with hard cheese topping is ready for the oven.

Straight out of the oven and ready to serve...

Lay the pie on a bed of spinach and serve with freshly boiled new potatoes or choose one of our rainbow salads.

Trans Fats

Healthy Trans Fats

We hear continuously that *trans* fats are bad fats. Not all trans fats are bad. Good *trans* fats are the natural fats found in some plants as they grow. They are also found in naturally reared cows, sheep, goats and in, non-contaminated, whole food dairy products.

Unhealthy Trans Fats – extracted from my book: Devils In Our Food, Page 60.

'The *trans* fat I am speaking of are the *trans* fats that are artificially manipulated and put into the food that is sold in supermarkets, fast food chains and other food outlets. These *trans* fats are **devils** in disguise and are found in 40 percent or more of the products on the supermarket shelves, in takeaway food outlets and small corner shops. *Trans* fat **devils** hide in:

- **Snacks:** potato chips of many flavours; some pre-cooked and pre-prepared popcorn including microwavable popcorn, tortilla pancakes, manufactured French fries, chips, and corn chips.

- **Commercially baked foods including:** cakes, biscuits and crackers (sweet and unsweetened), pies, frosting on unfrozen bought cakes including Danish pastries and biscuits and in commercially bought vegetable shortening.

- **Creamers and margarine:** non-dairy coffee creamers, margarines and some commercially produced bought foods containing creamers and margarine.

- **Commercially produced frozen pastry and dough:** frozen cakes of many types, tarts containing jam, apple, and other fillings; sausage rolls including meat pies, commercially bought dough, pastry, pizza, and doughnuts. *Trans* fats in doughnuts are one of the worst offending **devils** when it comes to the commercial manufacturing of food. They can contain up to 50 percent of *trans* fat as part of their ingredients.

- **Commercially manufactured and cooked food:** deep fried fast foods cooked in *trans* fats in deep fryers and bought at outlets include: fish and chips, pie and chips, doughnuts, hash browns and chicken nuggets. When a *trans* fat is used in cooking oil, it allows a longer shelf life and doesn't need to be changed or renewed as often.

- **Chocolate:** manufacturers of chocolate use *trans* fats in their production. Even expensive brands contain *trans* fats. *Trans* fat allow the chocolate bar to be sold as a bar of chocolate otherwise, we would probably buy the chocolate in a bottle and drink it as a drink! That said, the *trans* fat in a chocolate bar is doing no good to your health and wellbeing.'

DINNER

CHICKEN STOCK

Ingredients

1 dstspn organic olive oil
2 large organic onions
1 organic clove of garlic
2 organic medium carrots
2 sticks of organic fresh celery
2 Tsp Himalayan salt or
   organic rock salt or salt to taste
Organic, ground black pepper to taste
4 uncooked, organic chicken legs
1 litre of boiled water.

Cooking Time

1 – 2 hours.

Tips

Using fresh herbs can add to the texture and quality of any stock.

Once a stock is made, it can be stored in a sealed, tight container in the fridge or freezer.

Method

On a low heat:

- Heat oil in the pan
- Add the onion, garlic, celery, and carrots
- Allow to cook-down, then add the chicken legs
- Cover and allow to cook for about 30 minutes.
- Add the boiled water and allow to cook for a further 1 – 2 hours checking every 10 – 15 minutes, adding extra water if required
- Strain off the ingredients leaving a fine stock that can be used in many dishes, including pies. Freeze or store and use accordingly.

Extra vegetables and the chicken legs are added to the cooking and browning onions.

Cooking and browning onions, garlic, and celery.

Clear, strained freshly cooked stock for use anytime.

BEEF STOCK

Ingredients

1 dstspn organic olive oil
2 large organic onions
1 organic clove of garlic
2 medium organic carrots
2 sticks of fresh organic celery
2 organic parsnips
2 Tsp Himalayan or organic rock salt to
Organic ground black pepper to taste
2 organic beef spareribs
1 L of boiled water.

Cooking Time

1 – 2 hours.

Tips

Using fresh herbs can add to the texture and quality of any stock.

Once a stock is made, it can be stored in a sealed, tight container in the fridge.

Because of the density of the ribs, they may require longer cooking time.

Method

On a low heat:

- Heat oil in the pan
- Add the onion, garlic, celery, carrots, and parsnips
- Allow to cook-down
- Add the beef spareribs
- Cover and allow to cook for about 30 minutes
- Add the boiled water and allow to cook for a further 1 – 2 hours checking every 10 – 15 minutes, adding extra water if required
- Strain the ingredients off leaving a fine stock that can be used in many dishes, including pies
- Freeze or store and use accordingly.

Once the vegetables start to cook-down, add the beef spareribs

Use fresh, seasonal vegetables to make flavoursome stock which can last indefinitely in the freezer.

Readymade stock to use at anytime

SOUPS

Parsnip, lime, ginger, and organic coconut cream soup

Ingredients

2 dstspn organic olive oil
4 thinly sliced organic shallots
5g organic freshly sliced ginger
3 good sized, (not too big) thinly sliced, organic parsnips (with skin on)
1 organic, finely cut, clove of garlic
½ organic lime
1 Tsp Himalayan or organic rock salt
Organic, ground black pepper to taste
1 tin (400) ml organic coconut cream
1 L full cream, organic milk

½ litre water.

Cooking Time

15 – 20 minutes or until parsnip has softened.

Tip

By making larger batches of soup it can be frozen and used for future meals.

A light creamy soup with a delicious end tang of lime.

Method

- Wash and dry all vegetables
- Slowly heat the olive oil in a large saucepan
- Finely cut the shallots
- Grate the ginger
- Cut the parsnip into small cubes
- When heated, add shallots, ginger, garlic and parsnip
- Add salt and pepper to taste
- Allow to cook for about 5 minutes
- When cooked, add organic coconut cream and full cream milk
- Continue to simmer for about 10 minutes or until the parsnip is soft
- Remove from the stove and allow to stand for 5 minutes
  Squeeze ½ lime into soup and blend
- Blitz to a fine creamy soup. Garnish with parsley or fresh basil and serve
- Delicious when served with warm, sour dough bread.

Chickpea, coriander, and beef soup

Ingredients

2 dstspn organic olive oil
2 medium sized cut organic carrots
1 medium finely cut red organic onion
1 medium finely cut white organic onion
1 medium finely cut organic clove of garlic
1 medium, chopped organic swede
1 medium, chopped organic potato
2 sticks organic finely chopped celery
Coriander and parsley to taste
2 organic, organic beef spareribs
1 tin (drained) organic chickpeas
Himalaya or organic rock salt to taste
Freshly ground organic pepper to taste
4 L water

Cooking Time

3 hours

Tips use freshly bought or grown vegetables where possible. If the vegies are soft, cut off the top and tails and soak in cold water overnight. You will be surprised how tired vegies can become as firm and fresh as the day they were picked.

Where possible, leave all vegetable skins on. Of course, remove onion skins. The skins of both vegetables and fruit is where their nutritional value belongs.

Freshly cut vegetables cooking on the stove; while cooking in the oil, stir about every 5 minutes.

Method

- Heat olive oil in a large pan or saucepan
- Wash and dry all vegetables
- Cut and prepare onion and garlic
- Add to heating oil
- Once the onion and garlic are brown and crystallised, add the remaining vegetables, including the chickpeas
- Add salt and pepper to taste, allow to cook until softened (not too soft)
- Add the beef spareribs and allow to cook until the meat has changed colour
- Stir all ingredients every 5 minutes, do not allow to stick to the pan. Do this for about 20 minutes
- Add the water
- Allow all ingredients to cook for about 3 hours or until the meat is tender
- When cooked, remove the whole meat, and blitz the vegetables and water to make a delicious soup
- Slice the beef and use to decorate the soup
- Serve with freshly cooked wholemeal toast or a suitable organic made bread.

Hearty, healthy meals can cost as little as a dollar to make. The 4 spareribs were a little over $6.00 and the vegetables below $4.00. To give body to this soup, chickpeas add the thickener required. Serves: 8 – 9 people from one pot. The cost is a little over $1.00 per person. Garnish with sliced spare rib beef.

Tomato and green basil soup

Ingredients

2 dstspn organic olive oil
6 large organic tomatoes
3 sprigs fresh basil
1 medium red organic onion
5 organic shallots
1 Tsp Himalayan or organic rock salt or to taste
Organic ground black pepper to taste
1 cup of chicken or vegetable stock
Please see pages 70 and 71.

Cooking Time 45 minutes

Tips

A delightful hot soup for winter nights or serve hot or cold, garnished with a leaf or two of fresh basil.

To enjoy your soup, serve with freshly made damper or homemade bread.

Method

Remove the skin from the tomatoes

Put the tomatoes into a saucepan of water allowing the tomatoes to be covered. Bring to the boil and allow to stand for a few minutes. The tomato skin is easily removed once cool.

- Gently heat organic olive oil in a medium to large saucepan. When heated, add onion and shallots. Allow the onion and shallot to cook-down until they become transparent.
- Cut the skinned tomatoes into sections
- Add the tomatoes to the onion and shallots, allow to cook for 10 minutes or until soft
- Add finely chopped basil
- Add the chicken stock and allow to cook for a further 5 minutes.
- Blitz the ingredients, leave a little texture, this gives a visual appeal to your soup.
- Garnish with fresh basil and serve.

Celery, brown onion, and ginger soup

Ingredients

2 dstspn organic olive oil
1 medium brown onion
1 Tsp Himalayan or organic rock salt to taste
Organic ground black pepper to taste
2 medium organic potatoes
1 head of organic celery
1 clove of organic garlic
¼ tsp fresh grated organic ginger
1 cup freshly cut herbs:
Parsley, chives, coriander, and thyme. Leave some chives for the garnish
1 L of boiled water
1 cup full cream milk
Half cup of pre-made chicken stock
Please see pages 70 and 71.

Cooking Time Simmer for 1 hour

Tip

If your soup appears to be too runny: mix into a paste of 3 dsrtsp boiled water with 1 dsrtsp of organic, self-raising, flour or your chosen thickener. While stirring the paste, add to simmering soup mix.

Can be served as a cold or hot - garnish with chives.

Serve with organic, sour, rye bread.

Method

Wash, dry and cut all of the vegetables into small pieces.

- Slowly heat olive oil, add onion, ginger, and garlic, and allow to brown
- Add celery, potato and allow to cook until semi-firm
- Add fresh herbs and boiled water
- Cook for further 15 minutes
- Add milk and pre-made stock
- Allow to cool
- Blitz ingredients
- Allow to cool, add chives to garnish.

The mixed ingredients are cooking down to form the base of the soup.

Soup ready to eat and enjoy.

Cauliflower and organic Stilton cheese soup

This soup is such a winter warmer – if you like Stilton cheese, you will love this soup...

Ingredients

2 dstspn organic olive oil
1 large chopped organic red onion
1 small finely cut organic leak
1 finely sliced organic clove
1kg organic cut in chunks cauliflower
200g organic Stilton cheese
Himalayan or organic rock salt to taste
Organic ground pepper to taste
1L organic full cream milk
½ L water
Good handful of organic parsley

Cooking Time 20 minutes

Tip

Because of the milk and cheese ingredients, this is a soup that can easily catch or burn. Once the vegetables are cooked and the cheese and milk are added keep on the lowest heat possible.

Method

- Wash and dry all vegetables
- Gently eat the oil in the pan
- Once warmed, add the vegetables and parsley, and allow to cook until keeping the cauliflower firm about 5 minutes
- Add the salt and pepper to taste
- Slowly add the milk and water
- Allow to slowly cook for an extra 15 – 20 minutes or until the cauliflower has softened. Do not allow the cauliflower to overcook, you still need to have the 'crunch' in the flower
- Crumble the cheese then add to the cauliflower ingredients while they cook
- Allow to cool for 5 minutes
- Lightly blitz the ingredients keeping the grain of the cauliflower intact
- Serve with a garnish of your choice and with toasted sour dough bread.

Freshly cut vegetables cooking on the stove; while cooking in the oil, stir about every 5 minutes.

With all ingredients added, they slowly cook for about 15 minutes or until the cauliflower has softened but still has the crunch.

Spelt, organic bread has been toasted and accompanies this delicious soup. Garnish with Midgen Berry or your favourite herb.

CASSEROLES IN A PAN

Mushroom, beef, and red wine casserole in a pan

Ingredients

500g trimmed and cubed, organic selected steak
¼ cup organic olive oil
1 large red thinly cut organic onion
1 large brown thinly cut organic onion
2 thinly sliced organic cloves of garlic
1 medium size thinly sliced, red pepper
300g organic mushrooms
250g thinly cut sweet potatoes
Thyme, parsley, and herbs to taste
1 cup (half bottle) red wine
2 dstspn organic self-raising, flour for flouring the meat
Himalayan or organic rock salt to taste
Organic ground black pepper to taste

Cooking time 2 hours or until the meat is tender.

Tips

The meat may become dry as it cooks, from time-to-time, add a little water or beef stock to keep the ingredients moist. Please see page 71 for beef stock.

Method

- Cut the onion, pepper, and garlic into small pieces
- Heat the oil in the pan
- Add the onion, pepper, garlic, and herbs to heating oil
- Add salt and pepper to taste
- While these are slowly cooking
- Cut the meat into small cubes (not too big as the meat may take longer to cook)
- Flour cubed meat and add to the cooking onions and herbs
- Cut remaining vegetables into small cubes
- Add to cooking meat and the other ingredients
- Continually turn the cooking ingredients in the pan
- Allow to gently brown. (If you feel the ingredients are a little dry add extra olive oil)
- Add the red wine while stirring through the mixture
- Check regularly to make sure the ingredients do not dry out. Add extra wine and water if needed.

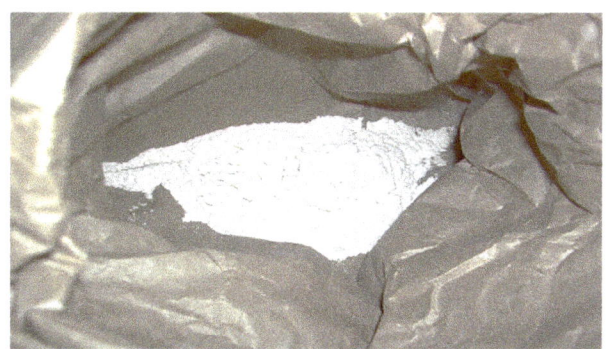

To save time and flour, put the flour into a paper bag (if available) and shake the meat in the flour to completely cover.

Onions, garlic, and herbs cooking down to create a delightful combination of flavours.

The time some meat takes to cook can be deceptive. For the fullness in flavour, allow meat to cook in its own time.

Once cooked, allow to stand for a few minutes, then serve straight from the pan or add to a serving dish.

Serve with hot, new potatoes, do not peel the potatoes, and or, as an optional, rye bread.

Chicken mushroom and white sauce – casserole in a pan

Ingredients

500g organic, cubed, breast of chicken
¼ cup organic olive oil
1 medium thinly cut organic white onion
1 medium thinly cut organic shallot
1 organic thinly cut clove of garlic
2 sticks sliced organic celery
2 medium size thinly cut organic carrots
2 dstspn organic self-raising, flour for flouring the meat
Himalayan or organic rock salt to taste
Organic freshly ground pepper to taste
1L full cream organic milk

Cooking time 30 minutes

Tips

Breast of chicken is a soft meat and will go stringy if cooked too long.

Method

- Heat the oil in a pan
- Trim and thinly cut vegetables, add to the heating oil
- Add salt and pepper to taste
- Add cut vegetables
- Cube and flour the chicken
- Add to cooking vegetables
- Gently stir the chicken and vegetables together allowing the chicken to brown
- Once browned, while stirring, slowly add the milk
- Continue to stir while the sauce thickens
- Allow to cook for about 15 minutes, and serve with your favourite vegetables.

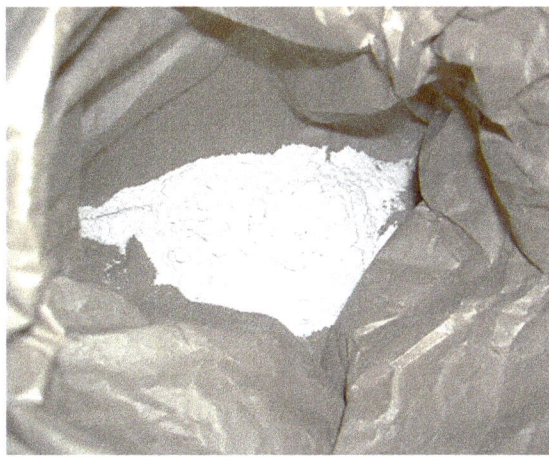

To save time and flour, put the flour into a paper bag (if available) pinch the opening together and shake the meat in the flour to lightly, cover. Make sure all meat is covered.

Occasionally stir the cooking vegetables prior to adding the cubed chicken.

 Slowly add the milk, this becomes thicker and forms a rich chicken and mushroom sauce.

 Garnish with parsley and serve with green vegetables and jacket potatoes.

Lamb, parsnip, and red wine casserole in a pan

Ingredients

400g fresh diced organic parsnips
400g organic diced lamb (buy whole piece and dice)
1 cut large organic red onion
1 cut medium organic clove of garlic
2 finely cut, small organic red capsicum peppers
3 – 5 finely chopped medium brown organic mushrooms
2 dstspn olive oil for cooking
Himalayan, or organic rock salt to taste
Freshly ground pepper to taste
2 dstspn organic white flour
1 cup organic red wine
1½ cups water.

Cooking Time 30 minutes

Tips: Parsnips have a natural sugar content, this comes through as they cook; depending on their age, they can become caramelised which adds a nice taste and texture to the meal.

Method

- Heat the oil in a pan
- Add onion, peppers, and garlic to the heating oil
- Allow to cook to develop their caramel coating
- Add salt and pepper to taste
- Add the diced parsnip
- Continue to move the vegetables around the pan as they cook; do not let them stand
- Add the mushrooms
- Coat the lamb with flour. (Preferably, use a paper bag), place the flour in the bag, add the diced meat, pinch the opening together and shake the meat and flour together until meat is fully coated.
- Turn up heat under the pan a little and add the floured meat to the cooking vegetables
- Stir the ingredients until the meat is slightly browned and reduce heat
- Add the wine, continue to stir all ingredients
- Slowly pour in the wine and water, continue to stir as the sauce thickens
- On a simmer heat, cook for 30 minutes or until the meat is tender.

Onions, clove of garlic and finely cut pepper in warmed oil cooking to soften and brown.

Cut parsnip added to the cooking vegetables.

Mushrooms are added as the parsnips start to soften and brown; move the ingredients continually while cooking.

*Put the meat in the flour, seal the top of the bag or hold tightly, shake bag to evenly cover the meat.

Add the meat to the cooking ingredients. Continue stirring while adding the wine and water.

A healthy meal served with 'cooked in their jackets' potatoes, baked parsnips and miniature egg plant. For greens we have used Kalettes – a brussel sprout and kale small vegetable. Garnish with fresh parsley.

*If available use paper bags where possible.

Fillet of beef, lamb, or goat – pastry-pocket roast

Ingredients

650g beef, lamb, or goat
2 good size organic shallots or small onions thinly cut
2 organic cloves of garlic thinly cut
100g organic chopped mushrooms
2 dstspn organic olive oil
Parsley to taste

Short pastry

1½ cups organic white self-raising, flour
½ cup organic olive oil
Himalayan, or organic rock salt to taste
Freshly ground pepper to taste
½ cup water, use water sparingly, measure as you go
1 beaten organic egg for brushing the pastry

Cooking Time: about 55 minutes for each 650gm

Tip: Fillet of meat should not be overcooked; when cut, it should be a slightly pink colour.

Method

- Warm the oil in an open pan
- Add the cut shallots and garlic and allow to gently brown
- Leave the meat as one whole piece trimming off any excess fat
- Put the meat in the pan and allow the meat to sear, turning each side about every 4 minutes. Do not cook through, the pastry will do this job
- Once seared, remove from pan, and allow to stand until the dough is ready

Pastry

- Blend the flour, olive oil and salt together rubbing it through your fingertips. When ready add the water to moisten the dough, do not over moisten
- Make the dough into a dough ball and allow to stand in the refrigerator for about 30 minutes.
- When rested, roll out the pastry into a square. The pastry needs to envelope the meat and cut mushrooms

Rub the ingredients until are well blended and resemble breadcrumbs.

Blend flour, salt, and olive oil, ready to blend together

Once the flour, salt and olive are rubbed evenly through, add enough water to moisten, gently knead into a dough ball, allow to stand in the refrigerator for about 30 minutes.

With the cooking shallots, sear the meat in an open pan, turning after about 4 minutes of cooking on each raw side. Once seared, leave to stand.

After 30 minutes of refrigeration, roll out dough ball into a square shape. Cover shape with cooked pan juices from the meat and shallots.

Spread the thinly, cut mushrooms and parsley over the cooked shallots on the pastry.

Place the meat on the mixture of mushrooms, parsley, and cooked shallots.

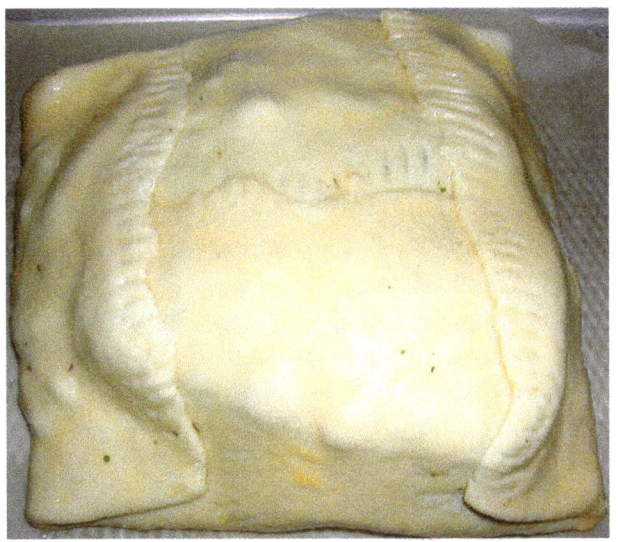

Wrap meat in the pastry and mushroom mixture envelope. Seal the pastry ends with the beaten egg and continue to brush all pastry with the egg.

Cooked and ready to eat – a delicious golden-brown envelope of tender beef.

Serve with freshly baked organic vegetables and organic baked potatoes in their jackets. Top with your homemade organic mushroom gravy.

Tasty organic mushroom gravy – perfect with many meals

Ingredients

5gm finely chopped organic fresh leak
200g fresh, organic finely chopped mushrooms
2 dstspn organic olive oil
Himalayan or rock salt to taste
Freshly ground pepper to taste
1dstsp white or wholemeal organic flour
½ cup to 1 cup of water

Cooking Time: about 5 minutes

Tip: If the mixture is not continually stirred the flour in the gravy mixture will become lumpy.

Method

- Put olive oil into a warm pan and allow to get hot
- When hot, cook the leaks until golden brown
- Add finely chopped mushrooms to heated oil and leaks and allow to cook through until tender
- Slowly add the flour to the cooking vegetables
- Continually stir the vegetables, and flour, pepper, and salt while you slowly add the water
- Cook until the mixture is thickened, then serve.

Once the olive oil is hot enough, add the thinly cut leaks.

Once the leaks are gold brown, then add the mushrooms and allow to cook through until golden brown.

Once the vegetables are cooked slowly add the flour while continually mixing flour and vegetable together, then slowly add the water while continually stirring. The outcome is a rich flavourful sauce without additives.

Goat, and red wine casserole with yogurt topping

A rich and delicious meal ideal for a cold winter evening

Ingredients

500gm diced organic or naturally feed goat meat
½ cup organic olive oil for cooking meat and vegetables
1 organic thinly sliced leak
1 small garlic clove
4 Bay leaves
3 sprigs coriander
2 sprigs fresh thyme
2 dstspn organic self-raising, flour
Himalayan or organic rock salt to taste
Organic pepper to taste
350g organic natural yogurt
½ cup of water
1 cup organic red wine

Cooking Time about 2 hours

Tip Goat is a game meat and, if old, may need extra tenderising, this can be done through pounding the goat with a meat mallet, wooden rolling pin or similar tool.

Method

- If the meat is on the bone, remove all meat, cut into small or diced sections
- Marinate with wine, raw leak, garlic, coriander, bay leaves and thyme (leave overnight)
- Remove all meat from the marinate and drain; keep the red wine juice
- Flour the meat, use a paper bag. Put the flour into the bag followed by the cut meat, hold the top of the bag while shaking the meat and flour together; make sure the meat is well covered with flour
- With the remains of the marinate, put into a pan, and gently warm, allow to cook for about 5 mins, remove from the heat
- Pour olive oil in the pan and allow to heat through
- Add floured meat, salt, and pepper to heated oil and allow to sear for about 5 minutes, no longer, the oven will do the cooking
- Put the cooked marinated herbs into a baking dish
- Once the meat is seared add the meat to the herbs in the waiting baking dish
- Add the water and marinated wine juices
- Cover with the natural yogurt
- Cover the dish with foil
- Bake in a warmed oven of 150° and cook until tender or about 2 hours.

Cut meat in red wine marinate.

 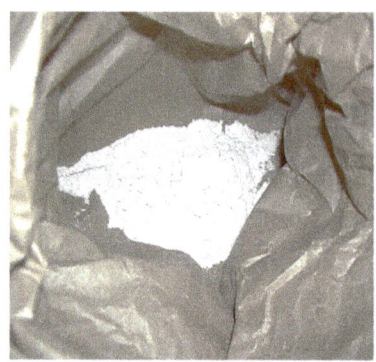 

After overnight marination, remove the meat, drain, and pat dry, this allows the meat to be floured ready for cooking.

Put the flour in a paper bag, holding open end closed, shake meat and flour well. This should cover all meat.

Cook the separated herbs in a separate pan for about 5 minutes, then spoon into the waiting baking dish.

On low heat, cook the floured meat until it has a golden-brown coating, about 5 minutes, promptly remove from heat, spoon meat onto herbs in the baking dish.

If you feel the mixture appears dry, add extra ¼ wine and ¼ cup of water before covering the meat and herbs with organic yogurt, cover with foil for baking.

Delicious baked goat's meat in red wine ready to serve.

Served with creamed sweet potato, deep fried (in organic olive oil), cauliflower, homemade mushroom gravy and lightly fried and browned mushrooms for garnish.

Fresh salmon with lime sauce

Ingredients

2 pieces organic or deep sea caught salmon left whole
2 dstspn organic olive oil
3 dstspn organic self-raising, flour
Himalayan or organic rock salt to taste
Freshly ground organic pepper to taste
½ Tsp organic Italian herbs

Cooking Time

15 minutes

Sauce

1 organic squeezed lime, (Keep ½ for squeezing and the other ½ for garnishing).
1 organic beaten egg yolk
3 dstspn organic, natural yogurt
Himalayan or organic rock salt to taste
Freshly ground organic pepper to taste

Tip

Serve with your favourite boiled or steamed vegetables or add some of the olive oil, deep friend vegetables seen on page 94.

Method

- Wash fish under fresh cold water
- Pat dry
- Spoon the flour onto a plate, add salt, pepper and Italian herbs
- Rub the flour into and over the complete fish
- Heat oil in the pan (the oil needs to be reasonably hot, wait to see a light blue cloud coming from the oil, then add the fish)
- After about 4 minutes, turn fish to cook on opposite side. Repeat this action on all sides of the fish until cooked and has a golden colour, outer crunchy coating.

Sauce

- Mix, by hand, the sauce ingredients. When smooth, garnish with a slice of lime.

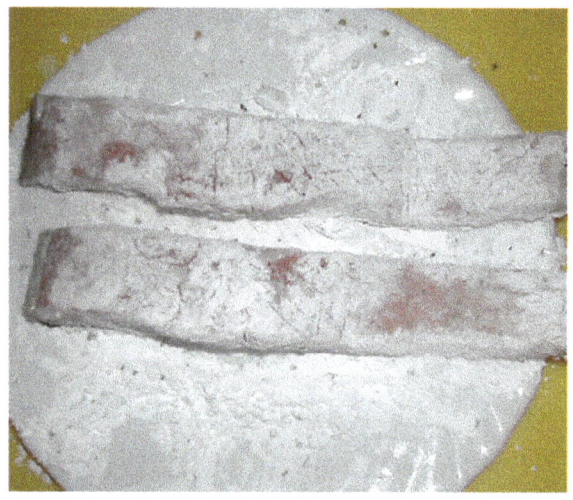

Freshly floured fish ready for frying.

This delicious lime sauce can accompany many different fish dishes.

A delicious fish meal served with steamed organic carrots. Brussels sprouts, freshly baked sweet potato, and lime sauce.

Alternative side dishes – vegetables - fried in organic olive oil – even children love them.

Other vegetables that are great to serve up with many meat and fish dishes can be deep-fried and lightly battered.

Batter Ingredients

3 dstspn organic self-raising, flour
3 dstspn organic self-raising, flour for dusting vegetables prior to dipping in the batter
I organic beaten egg
1 cup organic whole cream milk
Himalayan or organic rock salt to taste
Freshly ground organic pepper.

Method

- Wash and dry vegetables, peel if needed
- Dust the vegetables with flour
- Beat egg until the yolk and white are blended
- Add the egg mix to the milk
- Add the flour, salt, and pepper to the egg and milk mix and beat to make a consistent paste.

Cooking Time 5 – 8 minutes for each group of vegetables.

Batter ready for dipping the vegetables.

Batter needs to have a free-flowing cream consistency.

Frying medallions of organic potatoes.

Organic, golden-brown potato medallions.

Organic Parsnips cooked to golden-brown colour.

Organic runner beans are crunchy when served hot...

The flavour of organic red pepper is enhanced.

Organic carrots cut into slices are sweet and crunchy.

Organic sweet potato becomes sweeter when fried.

The crunchy cooked batter is lovely when fresh mushrooms are the last of the vegetables cooked in the hot oil.

Crunchy cauliflower just cooked - it's great with lime sauce. Please see page 92.

DESSERTS

Quick chocolate, dark cherry, and pistachio custard

Ingredients

6 large organic eggs
1½ L full cream organic milk
2 dstspn pure vanilla extract
2½ dstspn organic corn flour or your chosen thickener. (Please see page 7.)
2 dstspn organic chocolate powder or organic cocoa
2 dstspn organic honey
2 dstspn pure gelatin (not synthetic. Please see page 7).
50g dark, organic chocolate.

Topping

400g organic frozen or fresh dark cherries
2 dstspn pure gelatin
2 dstspn organic honey
1 cup organic fruit juice
100g freshly ground pistachio nuts.

Lining the cooling tin

For the next 2 recipes, line the cooling tin as shown on page 22.

Method

- Line a 23cm x 23cm (9") tin with cling BPA-free cling film. Make sure the film fits easily into the corners of the tin.
- Beat the eggs until whites and yolks are blended; once blended,
- Slowly add vanilla, honey, thickener, gelatin, chocolate powder, and milk to the egg mix and blend all ingredients
- Pour all ingredients into a large pan
- Turn on low heat to slowly heat through the mixture
- Continuously stir until mixture thickens
- Do not hurry the cooking time
- Pour into the lined cooling tin
- Prior to completely set, add broken pieces of chocolate to the top of the setting custard.

Preparation Time: 20 minutes

Cooking Time: About 20 minutes

Allow to stand and cool preferably overnight

Topping

- Slowly warm the cherries in a saucepan on the stove or in a bowl in the microwave
- Warm the fruit juice and gelatin together, continuously stir until the gelatin is completely dissolved
- Add the warmed cherries to the fruit and gelatin mixture
- When firm, evenly top the custard with the cherry and fruit juice mixture
- Sprinkle with crushed pistachio nuts, allow to set firm.

Tip: Thickener

Once chosen, mix your thickener and chocolate powder with a little milk to the consistency of a thickened cream and pour into the warming milk and egg mixture. (12 servings).

Partially set custard with chocolate pieces.

Top and evenly space the cherries, fruit juice and ground pistachio nuts over the custard.

Gently remove the cling film from under the base of the custard by placing a large spatula under the custard and sliding the film sideways.

Fresh strawberry base, honey custard and raspberry topped slice

Ingredients

6 large organic eggs
1½ L full cream organic milk
2 dstspn pure vanilla extract
2½ dstspn organic corn flour or your chosen thickener. (Please see page 7)
2 dstspn organic honey
2 dstspn pure gelatin (not synthetic. Please see page 7.)

Base

250g freshly sliced strawberries
2 cups freshly squeezed orange juice
1 dstspn pure gelatin

Topping

500g fresh raspberries
2 dstspn pure gelatin
2 dstspn organic honey
1½ cups organic apple or fruit juice.

Lining the cooling tin

For this recipe, line the cooling tin as shown on page 22.

Strawberries and orange juice base allowed to cool.

Method

Base

- Line a 23cm x 23cm (9") tin with cling BPA-free cling film. Make sure the film fits easily into the corners of the tin
- Slice each strawberry into four and line base of the tin
- In a small bowl, add freshly squeezed orange juice to gelatin, and slowly warm through until all gelatin is dissolved
- Cover the base of the strawberries with the warmed orange juice and gellatin and allow to cool until firm.

Custard

- Beat the eggs until whites and yolks are blended; once blended,
- Slowly add vanilla, honey, thickener, gelatin, and milk to the egg mix and blend all ingredients
- Pour all ingredients into a large pan
- Turn on low heat to slowly heat through the mixture
- Continuously stir until mixture thickens
- Do not hurry the cooking time
- Pour into the lined cooling tin.

Topping

- When the custard is cool, place the fresh raspberries over the top of the custard
- Warm organic apple juice and gelatin until gelatin has dissolved and slowly pour over raspberries and allow to set until the whole dessert is firm, preferably, overnight.

- **Tip Thickener**

These desserts have no preservatives but can be left in the fridge for 3 – 4 days. (12 servings).

Raspberry and organic apple juice topping

A super fresh dessert, ready to eat on a warm summer's evening

Cherry topped, honey, vanilla, gelatin, strawberry giant cupcake

This giant jelly cupcake makes a wonderful birthday cake and is great fun to make and present as a surprise

Ingredients

Custard

1 pint organic, whole cream milk
4 large organic eggs
1 dstspn pure vanilla extract
2 dstspn organic self-raising, organic flour or your chosen thickener (Please see page 7)
2 dstspn organic honey
2 dstspn organic gelatin (not synthetic. Please see page 7.)
½ cup off the boil water
Enough organic olive oil to grease the inside of both moulds

Fruit topping

370gm (if frozen, thaw before use, or fresh) cherries
2 organic oranges, squeezed
½ dstspn vanilla extract
2 dstspn organic gelatin
2 dstspn organic honey
¼ cup organic fruit juice.

Method

Custard

- Coat the inside of the moulds with organic olive oil making sure every surface is well covered, or, line with BPA-free cling film. If you use cling film, lightly grease the inside of the mould with organic olive oil, then push the cling film firmly into the shape of the mould with a pastry brush – make sure there are limited creases of the plastic in the mould shape
- In a large pan, gently warm the milk
- Beat the eggs together until blended
- Slowly add the gelatin to the beaten eggs
- Mix the organic self-raising, flour or your chosen thickener to form a runny paste; add the flour, honey, and vanilla to the beating mix
- When the mixture is well blended, add to the pan on the stove
- Slowly heat the custard through while continually stirring until the mixture thickens
- Once thickened pour into waiting mould.

Beat the eggs until the yolks and white are completely mixed together.

The beaten eggs with added honey, gelatin, and flour mixture.

Method

Fruit topping

- If you are using frozen fruit, thaw before adding the gelatin mixture
- Warm the organic fruit juice, when warm, add the gelatin continually stirring. The gelatin will become transparent when it is ready for use
- Add the vanilla to the thawed or fresh cherries
- Gently fold the cherries into the warm honey mixture
- Once mixed through add to oiled mould
- Place into the refrigerator and allow to set.

Preparation Time: 40 minutes

Allow to stand and cool: 3 hours or preferably overnight

Tip: Pure gelatin is good for growing bones, skin, gut, and bowel health and helps with the human digestive system. It is also great for children's growing and developing bodies.

Warming custard mixture. Do not leave the mixture to cook on its own. It needs to be continually stirred.

Both moulds and their contents are ready for the fridge. Test for firmness before removing and releasing from the mould.

Before setting, stickiness of ingredients within a mould can be avoided by lightly greasing the mould with olive oil, then lining the container with BPA-free cling film. Make sure the film sticks securely, eliminating as many folds within the film as possible. This is made easier by using the oiled brush to manipulate the film into the folds of the mould. This technique is only suitable for cold desserts.

Options: The custard base can be decorated with a variety of different seasonal fresh fruits.

The fruit top is added, and strawberry halves decorate the plate, use seasonal, organic fruits where possible.

Crowned with organic yogurt, this makes a great birthday treat.

Treats for Children

Learning By Doing...

Allowing children to watch as you work to prepare their food builds invaluable life skills in the child. Teaching children about the health value of the food they eat prepares them to only accept food that is good for their body, brain, and mind.

Once children have learnt these valuable lessons, they will willingly take care and enjoy their food, realising that 'junk' food and drink are poisons and will lead to ill health or sickness later in their lives.

Please note: sugar, in most traditional recipes, is used as a scaffold ingredient. A scaffold ingredient allows more flexibility with the other ingredients. It allows the mixture to rise, taste sweeter, be stickier and give it that moreish taste. Your brain loves it, but your body does not. Simply, your body does not know what to do with the leftover residue of empty carbohydrate and this is what makes us sick. Depending on how the sugar is extracted or produced, unwanted residue can stay in the body for a lifetime.

'In 1957, Dr William Coda Martin wanted to answer the question, *'When is a food a food and when is it poison?'* His answer: *'Medically: any substance applied to the body, ingested or developed within the body which causes or may cause disease.'[1]* Dr Coda Martin classified sugar as a poison *'because it has been depleted of its life forces: vitamins and minerals'[4] '* Extracted from my book, Devil's In Our Food.

Quick Healthy Eating Ideas for You And Your Family

---

[4] Dr William Coda Martin Michigan Organic News, March 1957, p. 3.

Children love to learn new things, why not be their teacher and go on the journey of learning together...?

Introducing Chrissy Cupcake

Please note: Chrissy Cupcake says: *'All children must be supervised when using electrical or cooking implements such as electric or battery operated beaters, stirring food in a saucepan on the lighted or heated stove or putting food into or taking from a heated oven.'*

Cup cakes

Basic honey, yogurt cupcakes

Ingredients

80g organic softened salted butter
1/3 cup organic honey
1 cup organic self-raising, flour
½ cup organic natural yogurt
1 Tsp pure vanilla extract
1 large organic egg
½ Tsp organic, non-aluminium baking powder.

Preparation Time

15 minutes.

Cooking Time

40 minutes or until golden brown.

Oven temperature

Heat oven to 180° before putting the cupcakes in to cook.

Tips

Chrissy Cupcake uses pre-cut paper cupcake cases to avoid using printed or inked cases. If you are thinking of having cupcakes for a child's party, why not create a case that is different and pretty?

Chrissy Cupcake says: for a lighter textured cupcake, please replace the yogurt with whole cream organic milk.

Method

- Beat butter, egg, and honey until creamed (if an electric beater is available, it's far easier to use than doing this by hand)
- Add the vanilla extract and yogurt
- When the butter, honey, egg. and vanilla are creamed, slowly add the flour, and baking powder

(To keep the mixture light, it is crucial to add the flour slowly)

- Beat until the mixture looks a light cream in colour
- Spoon into the cupcake cases and bake. Makes 12 cupcakes.

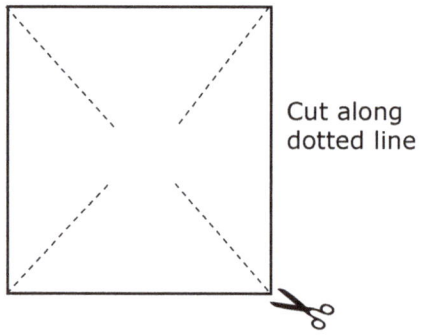

Cut along dotted line

Cut unbleached paper into the required size to fight the shape of the cupcake shell in the pan you are using.

Mixing butter, honey, and egg together.

The cupcake mix is spooned into the homemade cupcake cases ready for baking.

Golden cupcakes ready to eat or decorate.

With some fresh fruit for garnishing, basic cupcakes can be made to look delightful and fun to eat.

Plain, uncoloured paper cupcake cases are available either online or in some good cook shops.

Butter, honey, and rosette cream topping cupcakes

Ingredients

80g organic softened salted butter
1/3 cup organic honey
1 cup organic self-raising, flour
½ cup organic natural yogurt
1 Tsp pure vanilla extract
1 large organic egg
½ Tsp organic, non-aluminium baking powder.

Butter cream topping

60g salted, softened organic butter
1 organic egg yolk
1 dstspn organic honey
1 Tsp pure vanilla extract
2 dstspn organic arrowroot
1-2 dstspn organic milk if required.

Preparation Time

15 minutes.

Cooking Time

40 minutes or until golden brown.

Oven temperature

Heat oven to 180° before putting the cupcakes in to cook.

Tips

This creamy, buttery topping can be used to fill and top a range of dessert cakes – a handy resource when you want to avoid commercially made cream or dessert decoration products.

When buying arrowroot, check the ingredient panel at the side of the product. Many commercially made arrowroot products have sulphur dioxide (220) added as part of the ingredient. This should be **Avoided**.

Method

- Beat butter, egg and honey until creamed (if an electric beater is available, it's far easier to use than doing this by hand)
- Add the vanilla extract and yogurt
- When the butter, honey, egg. and vanilla are creamed, slowly add the flour, and baking powder

(To keep the mixture light, it is crucial to add the flour slowly)

- Beat until the mixture looks a light cream in colour
- Spoon into the cupcake cases and bake. Makes 12 cupcakes.

Butter cream

- Beat butter and honey until creamed (if you have an electric beater will make a smooth paste)
- Once the butter and honey are creamed, add the vanilla and egg yolk to the butter mixture
- Slowly add the arrowroot
- Cream all ingredients together
- Spoon a small amount onto each cupcake
- With the back of a fork, swirl to form a rosette shape.

Butter cream topping spooned on to the top of each cupcake.

Cream topped cupcakes...

Using the back of a fork makes it easier to swirl icing and cream.

Pretty butter and honey cream rosette cupcakes ready to serve.

Raspberry, jelly cupcakes

Ingredients

80g organic softened salted butter
1/3 cup organic honey
1 cup organic self-raising, flour
½ cup organic natural yogurt
1 Tsp pure vanilla extract
1 large organic egg
½ Tsp organic, non-aluminium baking powder
25g organic frozen or fresh raspberries.

Cooking Time

40 minutes or until golden brown.

Oven temperature

Heat oven to 180° before putting the cupcakes in to cook.

Raspberry juice

½ squeezed organic orange
1 Tsp organic gelatin
1 Tsp organic honey
5g organic frozen or fresh raspberries

Jelly and fruit topping

60g organic frozen or fresh raspberries
1 dstspn organic honey
1 dstspn gelatin
Raspberries to top
1/3 cup boiled water

Preparation Time

45 minutes.

Tips

Allow the cupcakes to be completely cold before adding the jelly topping.

Method

- Beat butter, egg, and honey until creamed (if an electric beater is available, it's far easier to use than doing this by hand)
- Add the vanilla extract and yogurt
- When the butter, honey, egg. and vanilla are creamed, slowly add the flour, and baking powder

(To keep the mixture light, it is crucial to add the flour slowly)

- Beat until the mixture looks a light cream in colour
- Spoon into the cupcake cases and bake. Makes 12 cupcakes.
- Allow the cupcakes to completely cool before adding any toppings.

Raspberry juice

- Squeeze the orange half
- Add the honey and raspberries to the juice
- Mix the gelatin into the orange, raspberry, and honey mixture and warm in the microwave
- Lightly brush the cupcake top
- Allow to stand while you prepare the crushed jelly topping

Jelly fruit topping

- Allow the raspberries to thaw if using frozen
- Warm the honey and stir through the fruit
- Add hot water or fruit juice to the gelatin and mix well
- Mix the gelatin into the raspberry and honey mixture and allow to set
- Once set, mash the topping with a vegetable masher or fork
- Spoon onto cupcake tops
- Add fresh raspberries or a fruit of your choice.

 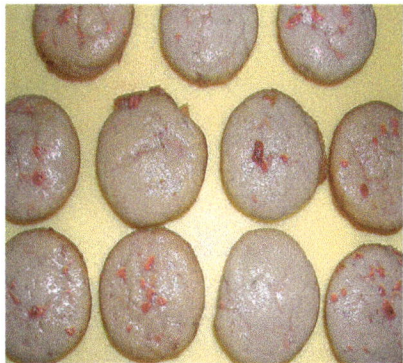 

Freshly baked from the oven. Allow to cool before decorating.

The cupcakes are coated with the raspberry juice prior to adding the jelly topping.

Jelly topping: If possible, prepare the jelly overnight.

The firm jelly is mashed with a vegetable masher this makes it look like jelly crystals.

Chocolate cupcakes

Ingredients

80g organic softened salted butter
1/3 cup organic honey
1 cup organic self-raising, flour
½ cup organic natural yogurt
1 Tsp pure vanilla extract
1 large organic egg
½ Tsp organic, non-aluminium baking powder
2 dstspn organic dark, drinking powdered chocolate or organic cocoa.

Cooking Time

40 minutes or until golden brown.

Oven temperature

Heat oven to 180° before putting the cupcakes in to cook.

Butter chocolate cream topping

60g organic butter
1 organic egg yolk
1 dstspn organic honey
1 Tsp pure vanilla extract
2 dstspn organic arrowroot
1 dstspn powdered organic chocolate drinking chocolate or organic cocoa
1-2 dstspn organic milk if required

Preparation Time

45 minutes.

Method

- Beat butter, egg, and honey until creamed (if an electric beater is available, it is far easier to use than doing this by hand)
- Add the vanilla extract and yogurt
- When the butter, honey, egg. and vanilla are creamed, slowly add the flour, powdered chocolate, and baking powder

(To keep the mixture light, it is crucial to add the flour and chocolate powder slowly.)

- Beat until the mixture looks a light cream in colour
- Spoon into the cupcake cases and bake. Makes 12 cupcakes.

Butter chocolate cream topping

- Beat butter and honey until creamed (if you have an electric beater, it will make a smooth paste)
- Once the butter and honey are creamed, add the vanilla and egg yolk to the butter mixture
- Slowly add the arrowroot and chocolate powder
- Cream all ingredients together
- Spoon a small amount onto each cupcake
- With the back of a fork, swirl to form a rosette shape.

Tip

Like all cakes, cupcakes are better served fresh on the day they are baked. However, these cupcakes can be made earlier and frozen. When defrosted, blitz in the microwave for 2 or 3 seconds, then add the toppings.

Just cooked chocolate cupcakes.

The tops of the cupcakes are removed ready for chocolate cream.

The tops are re-attached with the chocolate topping. Any remaining topping can be used to top the cakes.

Fruit topping of your choice. Here, Chrissy Cupcake has used golden kiwi fruit and fresh berries.

FREE of honey and sugar blueberry cupcakes

Juvenile onset diabetes or Diabetes Type 1 has increased over the years. More children are required to work with and manage this health condition. As a mother of a diabetic child, I can speak from my experience and know that some young diabetics miss out at birthday parties and on special occasions. While all forms of carbohydrate needs to be understood by the diabetic and the family, there are ways of giving these beautiful children a little treat every now and again. Remembering that even complex carbohydrate, through the body's system, converts to glucose.

Glucose is energy building and extracted by the human body from the natural foods we eat including fruit and vegetables. **Natural** glucose helps the brain to function and the body to be energised. Extracted sugar from cane or beet are empty calories that only contribute to ill health and weight gain and interfere with our hormone balance; this interference contributes to many obesity problems seen in the world communities today. Empty sugar calories can send a diabetic's sugar levels too high, which can lead to health problems.

Ingredients

80g organic softened salted butter
1 cup organic self-raising, flour
6 scoops pure Stevia
½ cup organic natural yogurt
1 Tsp pure vanilla extract
1 large organic egg
½ Tsp organic, non-aluminium baking powder.

Cooking Time

40 minutes or until golden brown.

Oven temperature

Heat oven to 180° before putting the cupcakes in to cook.

Preparation Time

45 minutes.

Tips

Allow the cupcakes to be completely cold before adding the jelly insert.

Method

- Beat butter and Stevia and egg until creamed (if you have an electric beater it is far easier to use than by hand)
- Add the vanilla extract
- When the butter, Stevia, egg and vanilla are creamed, slowly add the flour, milk and baking powder

To keep the mixture light, it is crucial to add the flour slowly

- Beat until the mixture looks a light cream in colour
- Spoon into the cupcake cases and bake.

Cupcakes straight from the oven. These cakes because of the lack of sugar or honey do not brown like other cakes, they do however, brown on the underside.

Sugar-free blueberry jelly filling for cupcakes and other cake fillings

Ingredients

250g frozen or fresh organic blueberries
½ squeezed organic orange
3 scoops pure Stevia
2½ dstspn pure gelatin
½ Tsp pure vanilla extract
1/3 cup boiled water
Organic cream or natural organic yogurt for topping

Preparation Time

45 minutes.

Setting time

3 hours or overnight

Tips

Allow the cupcakes to be completely cold before cutting in two and adding the jelly filling.

Your choice of organic fruit can be used.

Jelly fruit filling

- Allow the blueberries to thaw if using frozen
- Add the boiled water to the gelatin and mix well
- Add the Stevia and vanilla
- Add the fruit, while stirring the mixture
- Depending on the number of cupcakes you are going to make, line a 23cm x 23cm (9") tin with BPA-free cling film
- Allow the depth of your jelly to be about 1½ cm
- Once made, leave in the fridge to set
- Cut cooled cupcakes into halves
- Cut circles of blueberry jelly, add to bottom half of cake, then top with top half of cake
- Garnish with organic cream or yogurt and add a fresh berry for garnish.

You can use and shape for cutting out your jelly shape; here, I have used the round shape to fit the shape of the cupcake.

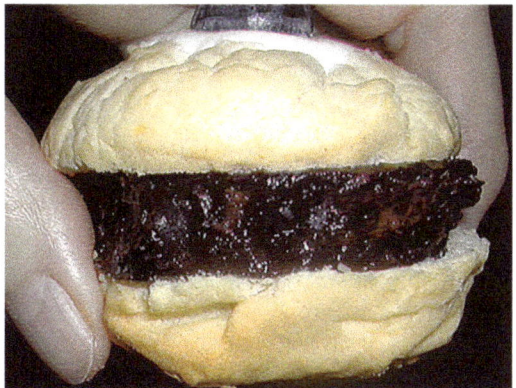

Compared to the original cupcake, these are lighter and drier in texture. They are a delightful change enjoyed by children and adults alike.

To add more fun, use different shapes for cutting the jelly.

Little treats for special people...

In my school life, I am still teaching children with diabetes, I know their journey and like many life-long health conditions, Type One Diabetes does not take a holiday or break. These cupcakes are topped with organic, natural yogurt.

Sugar is used in many bought cakes. As I have said, sugar acts like scaffolding in cooking. This, is why, many bought cupcakes and muffins have that sweet, gooey consistency. Sugar also allows the mixture to rise while baking. The sweetness of sugar works on your brain's receptors and once eaten requires more of the poison that we all call sugar. Sugar is an opiate and the more you eat, the more you will develop the craving for sugar.

Happy times chocolate and strawberry large cupcake – chocolate bottom

Ingredients

80g organic softened salted butter
1/3 cup organic honey
1 cup organic self-raising, flour
½ cup organic natural yogurt
1 Tsp pure vanilla extract
1 large organic egg
½ Tsp organic, non-aluminium baking powder
2 dstspn organic dark, drinking powdered chocolate or organic cocoa.

Cooking Time

The combined top and bottom cakes: 1 hour 10 minutes or until golden brown.

Preparation Time

45 minutes.

Oven temperature

Heat oven to 170° before putting the cupcakes in to cook.

Tips

Allow the cupcakes to be completely cold before adding the butter icing.

Chocolate butter filling

60g organic butter
1 large organic egg yolk
1 dstspn organic honey
1 Tsp pure vanilla extract
5 dstspn organic arrowroot
2 dstspn organic chocolate powder or cocoa.

Mould shape

All moulds are different. If you are using a shaped mould and have had problems removing the cake, once cooked, for baking, I use thin aluminium foil to line the shape.

1. Lightly grease the inside of the shape
2. Cut enough foil to allow the shape to be covered with one sheet
3. With a pastry brush, ease the foil into the shape
4. Once the foil is in the mould, with the rounded end of the handle of the brush, gently push the foil into the mould shapes.

Method

- Beat butter, egg, and honey until creamed (if an electric beater is available, it is far easier to use than doing this by hand)
- Add the vanilla extract and yogurt
- When the butter, honey, egg. and vanilla are creamed, slowly add the flour, powdered chocolate, and baking powder

(To keep the mixture light, it is crucial to add the flour and chocolate powder slowly)

- Beat until the mixture looks a light cream in colour
- Spoon into the mould and wait until the second half is ready to bake.

Chocolate butter filling

- Beat butter and honey until creamed
- Once the butter and honey are creamed, add the vanilla and egg yolk to the butter mixture
- Slowly add the arrowroot and chocolate powder
- Cream all ingredients together
- This can be done while both cakes are cooking in the oven.

Happy times chocolate and strawberry large cupcake – strawberry top

Ingredients

80g organic softened salted butter
1/3 cup organic honey
1 cup organic self-raising, flour
½ cup organic natural yogurt
1 Tsp pure vanilla extract
1 large organic egg
½ Tsp organic, non-aluminium baking powder
2 large or 4 small, fresh, finely chopped, organic strawberries.

Cooking Time

Combined top and bottom cakes:
1 hour 10 minutes or until golden brown.

Preparation Time

45 minutes.

Oven temperature

Heat oven to 180° before putting the cupcakes in to cook.

Tips

Allow the cupcakes to be completely cold before adding the butter icing.

Butter, honey topping

60g organic butter
1 large organic egg yolk
1 dstspn organic honey
1 Tsp pure vanilla extract
5 dstspn organic arrowroot
To decorate, use strawberries and blueberries or the fruit of your choice.

Method

- Beat butter, egg, and honey until creamed (if an electric beater is available, it is far easier to use than doing this by hand)
- Add the vanilla extract and yogurt
- When the butter, honey, egg. and vanilla are creamed, slowly add the flour, powdered chocolate, and baking powder

(To keep the mixture light, it is crucial to add the flour and chocolate powder slowly)

- Beat until the mixture looks a light cream in colour
- Fold the fresh strawberries into the mixture
- Spoon into the large cupcake mould container.

Butter filling

- Beat the softened butter
- Add the egg yolk and continue to beat until both are blended
- Add the honey and vanilla extract to the mixture, continue to beat
- Slowly add the arrowroot to the mixture
- Continue to slowly beat until all ingredients are thoroughly mixed
- Allow the cake to cool before adding butter icing
- Decorate to your choice.

Foiled mould. The right-hand side has the foil flattened into the shape. Do the same for the opposite side.

The uncooked mixtures ready for baking.

Cooked cakes directly out of the oven.

If needed, trim the top of the cake to flatten before adding chocolate filling. If you wish, add your chosen fresh fruit to the filling.

Cooled cakes ready for filling and topping.

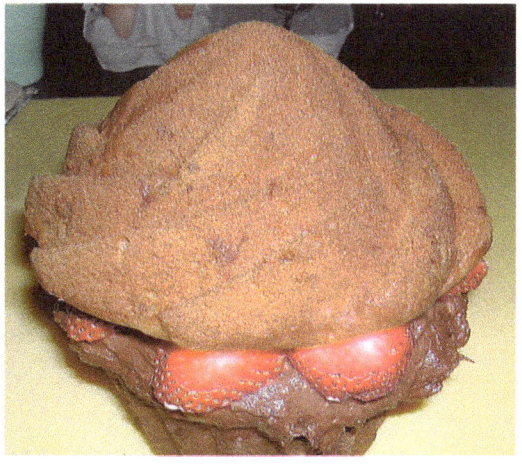
Add the top to the bottom. If the top has a slight rise, trim before adding the top to the bottom.

Cut cake ready to eat.
Because freshly made organic cake does not have the lasting time that cake bought at the supermarket has, (it has no preservatives in the form of humunctants) it can dry out within a day. If this happens, cut the portions, place in a microwave for 2 seconds, heat and eat – the cake retains the delicious flavours and is a great treat.

Happy times large cupcake – strawberry topped cake

A giant cupcake that will add laughter and fun to any celebration. If left in the open, the natural icing ingredients, do change slightly in colour.

Butter, pure vanilla extract, chocolate, and fresh fruit make this a delicious and different cake.

Introducing Saucy Sausage

In my years of teaching or preparing for my children's birthday parties or at a simple barbecue, I have not seen a child or adult refuse a nice-looking cooked sausage.

Sausages can be made from a variety of meats or different vegetables. They are a versatile and good meal when made with either organic or homegrown food.

Saucy Sausage delivers sausages to his customers

SAUCY SKINLESS SAUSAGES for Children's Snacks, Lunches and Parties

Sausages are an ideal snack or put into children's lunches.

Homemade sausages are full of goodness, and you know exactly what your child is eating. Following are a number of ingredient combinations that are affordable and makes healthy eating for all the family

With skinless sausages, you and your children are no longer eating the plastic wrapping that helps to keep supermarket or bought sausage together. The skins help to give marketing and selling appeal to the customer.

Tomato and cheeky beef sausages

Ingredients

500g organic minced beef
1 dstspn organic tomato sauce or 2 small organic fresh tomatoes
Pinch salt, not too much
1 Tsp organic Italian herbs
1 small organic finely cut shallot
1 organic beaten egg
½ cup organic plain flour
1 dstspn organic olive oil for heating in the pan.

Cooking Time

15 – 20 minutes

Tips

Sausages need to be a dry mixture this enables them to hold together while they cook.

If using fresh tomatoes, blanch in boiling water, this will allow the skins to be easily removed.

Method

- Heat oil in a pan
- Put the meat into a bowl
- Add beaten egg, tomatoes, Italian herbs, finely cut shallot and, by hand, thoroughly mix together
- Slowly add the flour while mixing all the ingredients.
- Roll the mixture into sausage shapes
- Put into heating oil and cook
- Turn the sausage frequently to maintain a round shape.

Children love to have fun when they eat, this is why we have developed the *Cheeky Sausage* character.

Saucy sausage enjoys dipping sauces when eating his food…

Serve with any number of the dipping sauces including tomato and others shown on page 127, you may even try some of your own combinations to make dipping sauces exciting and different!

Pork and apple cheeky sausages

Ingredients

500g organic minced pork
1 small organic, lightly stewed cooked apple
Pinch salt, not too much
1 Tsp organic Italian herbs
1 small organic finely cut shallot
1 organic beaten egg
½ cup organic plain flour
2 dstspn organic olive oil for heating in the pan.

Cooking Time

15 – 20 minutes

Stewing apples

- Core and peel the apple
- Cut into small pieces
- Gently bring to boil and cook for about 4 minutes or until tender
- Mash with the backside of a fork or with a potato masher. This will go in with your sausage mixture.

Tips

Apples are full of natural goodness which include: dietary fibre, antioxidants, vitamins, and a range of nutrients beneficial to good health. Apples also help to prevent heart disease, diabetes, obesity, and cancer. Apples help to prevent the accumulation of the free radicals which can and do build up in the human body's system.

Homemade cooked sausages can be cooked, frozen and stored and thawed when needed.

Ideal for parties, picnics, and school lunches.

Method

- Heat oil in a pan
- Put the meat into a bowl
- Add beaten egg, stewed apple, Italian herbs, finely cut shallot and by hand, thoroughly mix the ingredients together
- Slowly add the flour while mixing all the ingredients.
- Roll the mixture into sausage shapes about 5cm (2 inches long)
- Once the shape is formed, put into heating oil and cook
- Turn the sausage frequently to maintain a round shape.

Cheeky Sausage

Chicken, mushroom, parsley, and raspberry cheeky sausages with raspberry dipping sauce

Ingredients

500g organic minced pork and veal
6 mashed organic frozen or fresh raspberries
1 very finely chopped, organic mushroom
Pinch salt, not too much
1 Tsp organic Italian herbs
1 Tsp organic fresh or dried parsley
1 small organic finely cut shallot
1 organic beaten egg
½ cup organic plain flour
1 dstspn organic olive oil for heating in the pan.

Cooking Time

15 – 20 minutes

Dipping sauce

20g mashed, organic frozen or fresh raspberries
½ cup organic apple cider vinegar
1 Tsp pure gelatin
1 Tsp organic honey
¼ cup of off the boil boiled water.

Tip

Allow your child or children to experience different natural flavours, dress up the food making it look exciting and fun to eat. The more creative you become, the more your children will want to eat the food you prepare.

A great, different, and ideal treat for children's parties.

Method

- Heat oil in a pan
- Put the meat into a bowl
- Add beaten egg, raspberries, mushroom, Italian herbs, finely cut shallot, and parsley by hand, blend thoroughly together
- Slowly add the flour while mixing all the ingredients.
- Roll the mixture into sausage shapes about 5cm (2 inches long)
- Put into heating oil and cook
- Turn the sausage frequently to maintain a round shape.

Dipping sauce

- Combine the mashed raspberries with the organic apple cider vinegar and honey
- Combine the gelatin with the boiled water and mix until the two ingredients are thoroughly blended and transparent
- Mix the gelatin and water with the apple cider vinegar and raspberries
- Allow to cool and serve.

Turkey, thyme, basil, and blueberry cheeky sausages with blueberry dipping sauce

Ingredients

500g organic minced turkey
6 mashed organic frozen or fresh blueberries
Pinch of fresh or dried organic thyme and basil (not too much)
Pinch salt, not too much
1 Tsp organic Italian herbs
1 small organic finely cut shallot
1 organic beaten egg
½ cup organic plain flour
1 dstspn organic olive oil for heating in the pan.

Cooking Time

15 – 20 minutes

Dipping sauce

20g mashed, organic frozen or fresh blueberries
½ cup organic apple cider vinegar
1 Tsp pure gelatin
1 Tsp organic honey
¼ cup of off the boil boiled water.

Tip

Developing healthy eating habits in our children is the responsibility of adults. A child eats what it is fed and if a child develops unhealthy eating habits, the adults are to blame.

I often hear, '…oh so and so doesn't like that food.' It is understandable that a child does not like Brussel sprouts or some vegetables and that is because their tastebuds in their mouth are still developing. All children should be exposed to a range of different tastes and foods.

Method

- Heat oil in a pan
- Put the meat into a bowl
- Add beaten egg, blueberries, Italian herbs, finely cut shallot and by hand, thoroughly mix together
- Slowly add the flour while mixing all the ingredients.
- Roll the mixture into sausage shapes about 5cm (2 inches long)
- Put into heating oil and cook
- Turn the sausage frequently to maintain a round shape.

Dipping sauce

- Combine the mashed blueberries with the organic apple cider vinegar and honey
- Combine the gelatin with the boiled water and mix until the two ingredients are thoroughly blended
- Mix the gelatin and water with the apple cider vinegar and blueberries
- Allow to cool and serve.

Tip

Where possible keep children's food mild tasting but add different flavours as in dipping sauces to allow for different flavour experiences to develop.

DIPPING SAUCE IDEAS

Mango dipping sauce

20g blitzed organic frozen or fresh mango. If frozen, allow to thaw
½ cup organic apple cider vinegar
1 Tsp pure gelatin
1 Tsp organic honey
¼ cup of off the boil boiled water
¼ cup freshly squeezed organic orange juice.

Method

- Combine the mashed or blitzed mango with the organic apple cider vinegar, orange juice and honey
- Combine the gelatin with the boiled water and mix until the two ingredients are thoroughly blended and transparent
- Mix the gelatin mixture with the apple cider vinegar and mango
- Allow to cool and serve.

Mixed berries and dates dipping sauce

20g blitzed, organic frozen or fresh mixed berries. If frozen, allow to thaw.
2 dried or fresh organic dates blitzed
½ cup organic apple cider vinegar
1 Tsp pure gelatin
1 Tsp organic honey
¼ cup of off the boil boiled water
¼ cup freshly squeezed organic orange juice.

Method

- If the dates are dried, moisten in a small amount of warm water. When softened, blitz the dates to form a paste
- Combine the blitzed mixed berries with the dates, organic apple cider vinegar and honey
- Combine the gelatin with the boiled water and mix until the two ingredients are thoroughly blended and transparent
- Mix the gelatin mixture with the apple cider vinegar and mixed berries
- Allow to cool and serve.

Raspberry dipping sauce

20g blitzed, organic frozen or fresh raspberries. If frozen, allow to thaw
½ cup organic apple cider vinegar
1 Tsp pure gelatin
1 Tsp organic honey
¼ cup of off the boil boiled water
¼ cup freshly squeezed organic orange juice.

Method

- Blitzed the raspberries
- Add the apple cider vinegar and honey
- Combine the gelatin with the boiled water and mix until the two ingredients are thoroughly blended and transparent
- Mix the gelatin mixture with the apple cider vinegar and raspberries
- Allow to cool and serve.

Tip

You can make your own unique dipping sauces. They are so easy, why not introduce your children to this idea? You will be surprised at the different and tasty combinations you can make……!

Apple cider vinegar and honey dressing

Apple cider vinegar can make an interesting combination of either dressing or dipping sauces

1 Tsp organic honey
½ cup organic apple cider vinegar

Method

- In a small container, combine the apple cider vinegar with the honey and serve.

Saucy Sausage also likes to go for walks in the country

SAUSAGES for Children's Snacks, Lunches and Parties

Introducing Potato Pete and Sally Spud

To see the story book, Potato Pete Goes To Market, please see www.booksforreadingonline.com

Potatoes are a rich source of fibre, vitamins, and minerals. They are a great meal for children and adults, especially those potatoes that are cooked in their jackets.

Saying 'Hello' to Potato Pete and

Saying 'Hello' to Sally Spud

Despite what people say about potatoes, they are a nutritious, healthy, and staple food. They contain more potassium than bananas.

Some points to remember:

- Potatoes are low in sodium
- They are cholesterol free
- They are a good source of vitamin C
- They are also a good source of vitamin B6 and
- They, especially their skins, are a good source of fibre
- They are an excellent source of energy for children and they maintain the glucose balance in a child's system by providing good, sustainable energy for learning, playing, and having fun.

The nutritional value of potatoes outweighs the myth that potatoes are a fattening food. As with everything, potatoes need to be eaten in moderation.

Baked potatoes in their jackets can be cooked and left in the refrigerator ready to heat and serve up with your child's favourite topping. This is a meal that can be served up any time of the day...

Baked jacket potatoes – an exciting way to eat vegetables

Wash and score potatoes into 6 even sections. Do not cut through the potato.

Brush with pure organic olive oil, sprinkle with organic rock or Himalayan salt, sprinkle with organic Italian herbs.

Back in a hot oven 210° 40 – 60 minutes or until golden brown.

Baked potato served with crunchy organic bacon and fresh salad. You can add your own dipping sauce to these potato dishes.

Baked potato served with melted organic cheese and homemade organic bolognaise sauce.

Baked potato served with homemade sausages, organic carrot sticks and organic tomato sauce.

Baked potato served with pan-fried baby tomatoes, sliced boiled egg and organic cheese strips.

Dora Damper would like to make your acquaintance...
Dora Makes HONEY DAMPER BREAD

Dora Damper

Extracted from the book:

'Dora Damper Makes Honey Damper Bread'

Please supervise all children when teaching them how to cook.

The first recipe is an ideal way to introduce children to the art of healthy eating and preparing food.

Damper Bread

Damper bread is a sustainable health food. It has lasting energy benefits that equips a child, while at school, to concentrate on their lessons and allows them to enjoy the daily play that is needed by all children.

Damper is quick, affordable, and easy to make. It can be stored in the freezer, and a number of different combinations of ingredients, can be used to make the tastes different.

In the following pages, Dora starts with the basic, plain damper mix. She then move on to use dates, chocolate, pecan nuts, frozen raspberries, cheese and gives you other ideas – you may too, have many ideas of combining your child's favourite food....!

From Dora's experience she says, '....flour does change in its consistency. As the damper cooks, leave a good space around each to allow for rising and spreading.'

Mini plain honey damper bread

Ingredients

2 cups organic self-raising, flour
¼ cup organic olive oil
¼ cup organic honey
Sprinkle of Himalayan or organic rock salt
1/4 cup of water
¼ organic milk for mixture
¼ cup organic milk for coating.

Cooking time

20 minutes or until golden brown.

Oven temperature 170°

Tip

All flour seems to vary in weight, refining and texture. If the dough seems too dry, more water or milk to moisture the dough may be required.

Serve with organic strawberries, honey, and cream.

Method

- Put the flour in a large mixing bowl
- Sprinkle the salt into the flour
- Slowly add honey, olive oil, milk, and water
- Mix all ingredients to form a dough ball and lightly knead (not too much as the dough will become hard)
- Divide the dough into 12 small dough balls, space evenly onto a greased tray or line tray with unbleached, greaseproof baking paper
- Brush with milk
- Bake in the oven until golden brown and looking delicious to eat.

(Left) The dough mixed ready to be made into small dough balls.

Small dough balls on the baking tray prior to going into the oven.

Freshly baked honey damper bread ready for different topping, including fresh fruit or organic honey.

Mini raspberry topping damper bread

Ingredients

2 cups organic self-raising, flour
¼ cup organic olive oil
¼ cup organic honey
Sprinkle of Himalayan or organic rock salt
1/4 cup of water
¼ organic milk for mixture
¼ cup of milk for coating.

Raspberry topping

½ cup organic frozen or fresh raspberries
1 dstspn organic honey
¼ Tsp pure gelatin
2 dstspn off the boil water

Cooking time

20 minutes or until golden brown.

Oven temperature 170°

Tip

Once the damper is cooked allow to cool, then spoon in the raspberry topping and serve warmed – a treat at any time.

Method

- Put the flour in a large mixing bowl
- Sprinkle the salt into the flour
- Slowly add honey, olive oil, milk, and water
- Mix all ingredients to form a dough ball and lightly knead (not too much as the dough will become hard)
- Divide the dough into 12 small dough balls, space evenly onto a greased or line tray with bleached greaseproof baking paper
- Before baking, make a deep well in the top of the damper (this well is for the raspberry topping once baked and cooled)
- Brush with milk
- Bake in the oven until golden brown and looking delicious to eat.

Raspberry topping

- Blitz raspberries
- Add the honey and thoroughly blend
- Heat the water and add, off the boil, to the gelatin
- Thoroughly mix gelatin and water until clear and a light amber in colour
- Add gelatin mixture to raspberry and honey mixture
- Once cooked and cooled, spoon berry topping into the well.

Make a deep well in the middle of the dough ball before baking. I use the end of the pastry brush to make the well, it works and forms an easy shape.

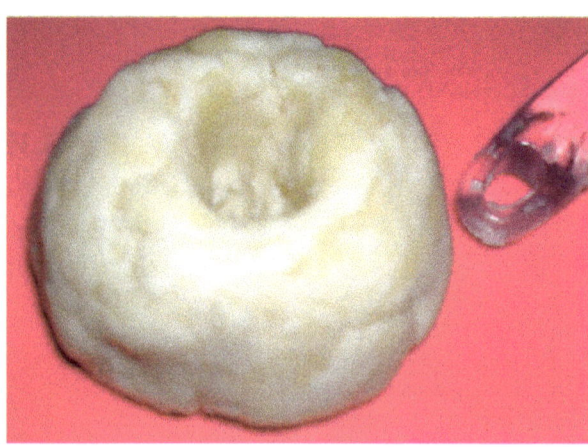

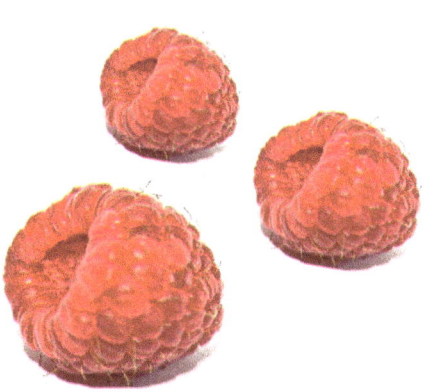

Mini blueberry damper bread

Ingredients

2 cups organic self-raising, flour
¼ cup organic olive oil
¼ cup organic honey
Light sprinkle of Himalayan or rock salt
1/4 cup of water
¼ organic milk for mixture
¼ cup of milk for coating.
15g organic frozen blueberries.

Blueberry topping

½ cup organic frozen blueberries
1 dstspn organic honey
¼ Tsp pure gelatin
2 dstspn off the boil water

Cooking time 20 minutes or until golden brown.

Oven temperature 170°

Tip

Once the damper is cooked allow to cool, then spoon in the blueberry topping and serve warmed – a treat at any time.

Method

- Put the flour in a large mixing bowl
- Sprinkle the salt into the flour
- Slowly add honey, blueberries, olive oil, milk, and water and milk
- Mix all ingredients to form a dough ball and lightly knead (not too much as the dough will become hard)
- Divide the dough into 12 small dough balls, space evenly onto a greased or line a tray with unbleached greaseproof baking paper
- Before baking, make a deep well in the top of the damper (this well is for the blueberry topping once baked and cooled)
- Brush with milk before baking
- Bake in the oven until golden brown and looking delicious to eat.

Blueberry topping

- Blitz blueberries
- Add the honey and thoroughly blend
- Heat the water and add, off the boil, to the gelatin
- Thoroughly mix gelatin and water until clear and light amber in colour
- Add gelatin mixture to blueberries and honey mixture
- Once cooked and cooled, spoon berry topping into the well.

Make a deep well in the middle of the dough ball before baking. I use the end of the pastry brush to make the well, it works and forms an easy shape. Please see page 134.

Mini black currant, sultana, and honey damper bread

Ingredients

2 cups organic self-raising flour
¼ cup organic olive oil
¼ cup organic honey
Sprinkle of Himalayan or rock salt
1/4 cup of water
¼ organic milk for mixture
¼ cup of milk for coating.
30g (half cup) organic mixed currants and sultanas.

Cooking time 20 minutes or until golden brown.

Oven temperature 170°

Tip

If the fruit seems dry, soak in warm water for 1 hour before adding it to the dough mix.

Method

- Put the flour in a large mixing bowl
- Sprinkle the salt into the flour
- Add the honey
- Add the currants and sultanas
- Mix with your hands to make sure the ingredients are evenly blended through the mixture
- Slowly add the water and milk
- Mix all ingredients to form a dough ball and lightly knead (not too much as the dough will become hard)
- Divide the dough into 12 small dough balls, space evenly onto a greased or line tray with greaseproof baking paper
- Brush with milk before baking
- Bake in the oven until golden brown and looking delicious to eat.

Damper bread is ideal for children and older student lunches.
Because it has sustainable energy built into the ingredients and is a complex carbohydrate.

Mini date, fresh banana, cherry, and honey damper bread

Ingredients

2 cups organic self-raising, flour
¼ cup organic olive oil
¼ cup organic honey
Sprinkle of Himalayan or rock salt
1/4 cup of water
¼ organic milk for mixture
¼ cup of milk for coating.
½ fresh mashed organic banana
20g fresh or organic frozen cherries
2 thinly cut organic fresh or dried dates.

Cooking time 20 minutes or until golden brown.

Oven temperature

170°

Tip

Cut in two and serve with organic butter.

Method

- Put the flour in a large mixing bowl
- Sprinkle the salt into the flour
- Add the honey
- Add the cherries, dates and mashed banana
- Mix with your hands to make sure the ingredients are evenly blended through the mixture
- Slowly add the water and milk
- Mix all ingredients to form a dough ball and lightly knead (not too much as the dough will become hard)
- Divide the dough into 12 small dough balls, space evenly onto a greased or line a tray with unbleached greaseproof baking paper
- Brush with milk before baking
- Bake in the oven until golden brown and looking delicious to eat.

Tip

Damper is a great food that can be served at children's parties, barbecues, and other social gatherings.

Mini organic very chocolate and pecan nut damper bread

Ingredients

2 cups organic self-raising, flour
¼ cup organic olive oil
¼ cup organic honey
Sprinkle of Himalayan or rock salt
1/4 cup of water
¼ organic milk for mixture
2 dstspn organic chocolate powder or cocoa
½ cup crushed pecans
¼ cup of milk for coating.
Enough whole pecan nuts to top each damper.

Cooking time 20 minutes or until golden brown.

Oven temperature

170°

Optional: Chocolate butter topping

30g organic softened butter
1 large organic egg yolk
1 dstspn organic honey
1 Tsp pure vanilla extract
3 dstspn organic arrowroot
2 dstspn organic chocolate powder or organic cocoa.

Tip

If you and your family like the combination of chocolate and pecan nuts, this is a damper you will love.

An option if you are unsure about nuts and nut allergies, leave out the pecan nuts and enjoy the very chocolate damper as a treat.

Method

- Put the flour in a large mixing bowl
- Sprinkle the salt into the flour
- Add the honey
- Sprinkle the chocolate powder or cocoa into the mixture
- Slowly add the water and milk
- Mix all ingredients to form a dough ball and lightly knead (not too much as the dough will become hard)
- Divide the dough into 12 small dough balls, space evenly onto a greased or line tray with unbleached greaseproof baking paper
- Brush with milk before baking
- Bake in the oven until golden brown and looking delicious to eat.

Chocolate butter topping

- Beat the softened butter
- Add the egg yolk and continue to beat until both are blended
- Add the honey and vanilla extract to the mixture, continue to beat
- Slowly add the arrowroot and chocolate powder or cocoa to the mixture
- Continue to slowly beat until all ingredients are thoroughly mixed.
- Allow the damper bread to cool before adding butter icing.

Tip

If the butter topping appears too moist, add extra arrowroot until reaching desired firmness.

Damper bread is a great way to introduce children to cooking good, whole food. While they learn simple food techniques, they gain valuable life skills.

Mini cheesy damper bread

Ingredients

1 cup organic self-raising, flour
Sprinkle of Himalayan or rock salt
10g shredded hard cheese (Grana Padano or similar)
1/3 cup organic olive oil
1/3 cup of water
¼ cup of milk for coating.

Cheese topping

Sprinkle Grana Padano or similar cheese.

Cooking time 20 minutes or until golden brown.

Oven temperature 170°

Tip

This flavoursome cheese damper bread is designed for the child palate – some cheese may be too strong in flavour.

Method

- Put the flour in a large mixing bowl
- Sprinkle the salt into the flour
- Add the cheese, mix with your hands
- Slowly add the water
- Mix all ingredients to form a dough ball and lightly knead (not too much as the dough will become hard)
- Divide the dough into 12 small dough balls, space evenly onto a greased or line tray with unbleached greaseproof baking paper
- Brush with milk before baking
- Sprinkle with grated cheese
- Bake in the oven until golden brown and looking delicious to eat.
- Remove from the oven, allow to cool and then, if you wish, add extra grated cheese for extra flavour.

Children's Lunches from Your Kitchen

Lightly gingered biscuits, cheesy straws, homemade sausage, bread, and fresh organic fruit and vegetables give your child and children sustainable energy throughout the school day. These foods also help them to enjoy their playtime and other good times in their lives.

Biscuits

Cheesy straw biscuits – ideal for school lunches

Ingredients

1 cup organic plain flour
1 cup organic self-raising, flour
Salt to taste – not too much
75g grated Grana Padano or similar cheese
½ cup organic olive oil
¼ cup water
¼ cup milk for coating

Cheese topping

25g Grana Padano cheese for topping
Sprinkle Grana Padano or similar cheese.

Cooking time 20 – 25 minutes or until golden brown.

Oven temperature 180°

Tip

These very tasty cheese straws can be stored in a sealed container and kept in the fridge. Great treats for school lunches, barbecues, or afternoon nibbles.

Method

- Warm the oven to 180°
- Cover baking tray with unbleached baking paper
- Put all of the dry ingredients into a bowl, by hand, mix together
- Add the oil while mixing the ingredients
- Roll out pastry into thin sheet (5mm or ¼ inch thick)
- Cut into thin strips about (75mm or 2½ inch long strips x 20 mm or ¾ inch wide)
- Brush with the milk
- Twist when placing them on the baking tray
- Bake until golden brown.

Just baked and ready to eat.

Honey, ginger biscuits

Ingredients

¾ cup organic self-raising, flour
¾ cup organic plain flour
½ cup organic honey
1 Tsp organic dried ginger
½ cup organic olive oil
Water to moisten.

Cooking Time 20 – 25 minutes or until golden brown.

Oven temperature 180° for 20 – 25 minutes

Tip

Freshly grated organic ginger may be a little strong in taste for children. It may also burn a child's mouth. Organic dried ginger is milder in taste and good for adding a depth of flavour to biscuits and cakes.

Method

- Warm the oven to 180°
- Put all dry ingredients into a bowl, by hand, mix together
- Add the oil and blend the ingredients
- Add a little water if the mixture appears to be too dry
- Roll out mix into 7 – 10 mm or ¾ inch thick
- Cut into desired shape: square, round or as you wish
- Cover baking tray with unbleached baking paper
- Place biscuit shapes on the tray
- Brush with the milk
- Bake until golden brown.

Ginger biscuits are a great treat served at any time: plain or decorated.

BREADS

SODA BREAD

Light, organic soda bread with yogurt and oats

Ingredients

1 cup organic Bakers' flour
1 cup organic plain flour
1 cup organic self-raising, flour
1 cup organic oats
½ Tsp organic bicarbonate of soda
Organic Himalayan or organic salt to taste – not too much
20g organic salted butter
½ cup organic yogurt
½ cup organic full cream milk
½ cup warm water.

Milk topping

¼ cup whole cream organic milk.

Cooking Time 35 – 40 minutes or until golden brown.

Oven temperature 180°

Tip

The bread is ready if the sound is hollow when you knock on the bottom of the loaf.

Method

- Warm the oven
- In a large mixing bowl add the different flour, oats, and bicarbonate of soda
- Mix all ingredients together
- Rub the butter with your fingertips through the different flour and oats, when well rubbed,
- Add the milk, yogurt, and water
- Allow to stand for 10 minutes
- Pat into shape
- Place loaf on unbleached greaseproof paper on the baking tray
- Pat with milk
- Bake in the oven until cooked or golden brown.

A deliciously light bread that can be enjoyed with different cheeses, soups or put in the children's lunch packs.

RYE HONEY BREAD

Rye bread with a difference

Ingredients

1½ cups organic rye flour
2¾ cups organic wholemeal self-raising, flour
5 Tsp homemade yeast
1¼ cups water
3 Tsp Himalayan or organic rock salt
4 Tsp organic honey

Cooking Time 35 – 40 minutes or until golden brown.

Oven temperature 180°

Tip

Homemade yeast is easy to make.

Ingredients – Homemade yeast

3 dstspn self-raising, wholemeal organic flour
4 dstspn warm water
1 dstspn natural organic yogurt

Method

- Warm the oven
- In a large mixing bowl add the different flour, oats, and bicarbonate of soda
- Mix all ingredients together
- Rub, with your fingertips, the butter through the different flour and oats; when well rubbed,
- Add the water, honey, and yeast
- Make into a large dough ball
- Cover with tea towel while standing
- Allow to stand for 3 hours
- Remove from the standing bowl and knead the dough for 10 minutes
- Allow to stand for a further hour
- Remove from bowl, lightly knead
- Divide the dough into of 4 smaller dough balls
- Place the dough balls onto unbleached greaseproof paper on a baking tray
- Pat each dough ball with milk
- Sprinkle lightly with flour
- Bake in the oven until cooked or golden brown.

Homemade yeast – Method

- Use an airtight jar to store your yeast
- Place all ingredients into the jar
- Stir until all of the ingredients are well mixed
- Securely place the lid on the jar and make sure it is airtight
- Store in the refrigerator until use
- The yeast will start to grow a darker top skin and when the lid is removed will have a nice fresh yeasty smell.

This recipe makes 4 smaller loaves.

920 – L-cysteine monohydrochloride mentioned on page 8, is a food additive used in many bought dough products. This additive is produced from bird feathers, animal hair, including hog hair. If from China, human hair is also used in this additive. Is widely used as a food supplement. Is also used as a food enhancer. Is used in flour as it stabilises the structure of leavened bread. Is known as a neurotoxin. Seek medical help before consumption of this product. This is a synthesized, unbound chemical which is widely used in food manufacturing and the food industry.

Tip

When you use some of your yeast, replace it with 1 or 2 dstspn of fresh wholemeal self-raising, flour and 2 dstspn of water. Mix, add to fermenting yeast, secure the lid, put back into the fridge for storage. When using the yeast, remove from the fridge and allow to warm to room temperature.

This doughball makes 4 medium-sized loaves.

The remaining 4 loaves can be frozen or wrapped and sealed and kept in the fridge. If left too long, it may develop a mould, similar, to its yeast product.

This tasty bread is a great with homemade soup and rainbow salads.

TARTS

Fruit Tarts

Raspberry, honey and almond pastry fruit tarts with vanilla custard and fresh fruit topping

PASTRY

Ingredients

½ cup organic plain flour
½ cup organic self-raising, flour
½ cup organic almond meal
50g organic un-salted butter 1 dstspn organic
¼ Tsp Himalayan or organic rock salt
1 Tsp pure vanilla extract
¼ - ½ cup boiled water to moisten pastry mixture
Olive oil to brush pastry tin shells.

Cooking Time 15 – 20 minutes or until golden brown and crisp to touch.

Oven temperature 180°

Fruit filling

100g organic frozen raspberries
1 dstspn organic honey
2 Tsp pure gelatin
½ pure organic fruit juice.

Custard

3 large organic eggs
1 Tsp pure vanilla extract
¼ cup off-the-boil water
1 dstspn organic honey 2 dstspn (20g) organic arrowroot or your chosen thickener.

Method - Pastry

- Warm the oven
- Put the dry ingredients into a large mixing bowl and by hand mix together
- Add the salt, honey, and butter
- Rub the ingredients through your fingertips to blend
- Add enough water to make a firm dough
- Roll out the pastry, cut into 12 cases to fit baking tin shape. (Do not make the cases too thick)
- Brush the pastry tin shells with oil
- Put cut pastry into place in the tin
- Bake in the heated oven.

Method - Fruit filling

- If frozen, defrost the berries in the microwave
- Warm the juice, add the gelatin. Make sure all gelatin is dissolved
- Add the raspberries to the gelatin and juice and gently stir together. Try not to bruise the fruit
- Spoon evenly into all 12 pastry cases.

Method - Custard

- Beat the eggs together until blended
- Slowly add the gelatin to the boiled water, when clear,
- Add the gelatin to the beaten eggs
- Add the honey and vanilla extract to the egg mixture
- Mix the organic self-raising, flour, or your chosen thickener to form a runny paste; add the flour, honey, and vanilla to the mixture as you beat
- When the mixture is well blended, add to the pan on the stove
- Slowly heat the custard while continually stirring until the mixture thickens
- Once thickened, allow to cool, not too cold, then spoon onto fruit-based tarts
- Top with fresh organic fruit of your choice.

Baked pastry shells removed from the baking tin and left to cool.

Pastry shells with raspberry fruit mix.

These are a great fruit tart to bring out with Christmas drinks, at birthdays or for a special occasion.

Honey, apple, and black currant tarts with meringue topping – Meringue without sugar

Ingredients

Honey pastry

½ cup plain organic flour
1 cup organic self-raising, flour
1 dstspn organic honey
¼ cup organic olive oil
50g organic un-salted butter
¼ Tsp Himalayan or organic rock salt
1 Tsp pure vanilla extract
¼ - ½ cup boiled water to moisten pastry mixture
Olive oil to brush pastry tin shells.

Cooking Time 15 – 20 minutes or until golden brown and crisp to touch.

Oven temperature 180°

Fruit filling

3 peeled and cored organic medium sized Granny Smith apples
½ cup organic black currants
1 dstspn organic honey
2 Tsp pure gelatin
¾ cup of water for cooking the apples and black currants.

Meringue topping

3 egg whites
1 dstspn organic corn flour
1 Tsp pure vanilla extract
4 spoons natural stevia. Please see page 2.

Tip

Natural Stevia can be bought at some good organic food stores or online.

Method

Pastry

- In a large mixing bowl, add the flours, honey, butter, vanilla and the ¼ cup of olive oil. Rub together through your fingertips until all ingredients resemble fine breadcrumbs
- Add enough water to make a dough ball. Do not handle too much as the consistency of the dough will change and may become hard
- Roll out dough ball to cut and line 12 pastry tin shapes. Use a tart tin, not a muffin tin.
- Cook in the oven until the pastry has a golden-brown edge and is crisp to touch.

Fruit filling

- If the fruit filling seems too wet, drain but keep a little fruit juice for mixing with the gelatine.
- You need a thick fruity base for these tarts
- Combine the cooked fruit with the honey
- Mix the gelatin with a little of the warmed apple juice, combine with cooked fruit and honey, spoon into cooked pastry shells.

Meringue

- In a large mixing bowl, beat the egg whites until peaks form
- Slowly fold in the corn flour, stevia and vanilla extract, do not beat.
- Spoon meringue onto tart tops
- Return to hot oven 200° for 3 - 5 minutes or until the meringue has golden-brown edges.

Just baked pastry shells allowed to cool.

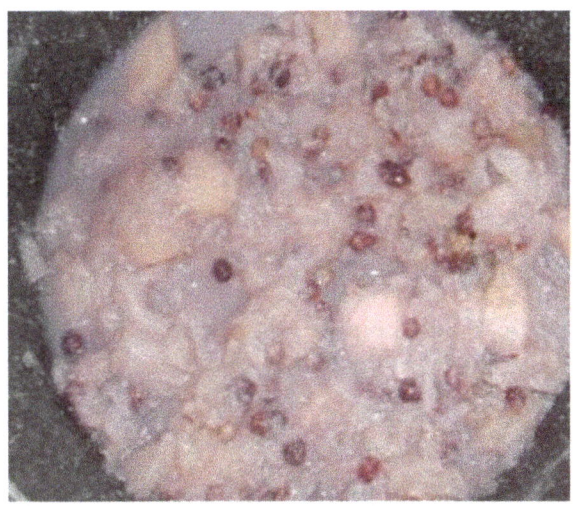
Cooked apple and black currant fruit before being drained of its juice.

Cooled shells with the apple and black currant filling.

> **Why is sugar a toxin?**
>
> Sugar in its natural form is not harmful to the human system; **it is the refinement of sugar that makes it toxic.**

Baked and ready for serving. The meringue in these little gems seems to last and stay firm when stored in the fridge.

Festive feasting

If you want to create the 'WOW' factor in your desserts, why not try these!

The healthy ingredients will amaze people when you tell them, *'there is no added sugar, they are all made from 100 percent organic ingredients….'*

Raspberry, pecan flan with vanilla creamed custard topping

Ingredients

Pastry

1 cup organic plain flour
½ cup organic self-raising, flour
1 Tsp organic almond meal (optional)
½ Tsp Himalayan or organic rock salt
1 dstspn organic honey
1 Tsp pure vanilla extract
¼ cup organic olive oil
¼ - ½ cup boiled water to moisten pastry mixture.

Filling

400g thawed organic raspberries
1 dstspn organic honey
1 Tsp pure vanilla extract
¼ pure organic orange or apple juice if required
25g organic pecan nuts (enough to cover the raspberry base).

Custard

3 large organic eggs
1 dstspn organic honey
1 Tsp pure vanilla extract
1 L organic whole cream milk
1½ dstspn arrowroot thickener
2 dstspn extra milk to make the milk and arrowroot paste

Cooking Time 20 – 25 minutes or until golden brown edges are seen on the edge of the pastry.

Oven temperature 160°

Tip

Do not hurry the making or baking of this delightful flan – enjoy the moments of creation.

Method

- Mix all dry pastry ingredients in a large mixing bowl
- Add honey, olive oil and vanilla extract
- Rub through your fingers until the ingredients are thoroughly together resembling a light breadcrumb texture
- Add enough water to form a dough
- Cover and leave to stand while the raspberry fruit base is prepared.

Fruit filling

- Slowly thaw the raspberries either on the stove or in the microwave (do not allow the raspberries to boil
- Add the vanilla extract and honey
- If needed, add the pure fruit juice
- Evenly line the bottom of the uncooked pastry base with the raspberry mixture
- Place, face down, the pecan nuts starting at the edge
- Bake in the oven until the pastry edge appears as light golden-brown 20 – 25 minutes.

Custard topping

- In a pan, slowly warm the milk
- By hand, mix the arrowroot with a little milk to make a paste
- Add the honey and vanilla extract to the paste and mix thoroughly
- As the milk warms, while stirring, add the paste
- Continue to stir the custard as it starts to thicken
- When thickened, add the custard to the cooked base of raspberries and pecan nuts
- Top with your favourite fruit of the season
- Serve cold and straight from the fridge.

Frozen raspberries need to be gently thawed. Like fresh raspberries, their flavour is delicate, and this should be respected.

Pecan nuts create a delicate flavour combination when incorporated with raspberries.

This delightful flan will win hearts every time it is served.

Rose, lemon, and orange bundt cake

Ingredients

3 large organic eggs
2½ cups organic self-raising, flour
1 Tsp non-aluminium baking powder
¼ Tsp Himalayan or organic rock salt
80g soft salted organic butter
3 dstspn freshly squeezed organic orange juice
3 dstspn organic rose water
3 dstspn organic orange water
2 dstspn pure organic vanilla essence
Zest of 1 orange.

Cooking Time 55 minutes or until golden brown.

Oven temperature 170°

Glazing

½ cup organic honey
¼ freshly squeezed orange juice

Topping

Choose fresh fruit of your choice.

Tips

All ovens work differently. Getting to know how hot the oven becomes is part of the journey of home baking. Your eyes are the most efficient way of telling if a cake is cooked or not. Also, the narrow sharp knife test. Insert a long narrow knife into the cake, if it comes out clean, the cake is cooked.

Please note: I add the wet and dry ingredients slowly, then blend a little and start the same process again. This way I am assured that lumps will not form in the mix.

Method

- Oil the mould making sure that every part is well covered
- Beat eggs and butter together
- When beaten, add tablespoon by table spoon the baking powder, flour, salt, rose and orange water with orange juice, vanilla essence, and orange zest
- Slowly beat together until all ingredients are blended
- Slowly pour the mixed ingredients into the oiled mould
- Tap the mould on the bench to make sure the ingredients have settled into the shape of the mould
- Put into the heated oven to cook
- When golden brown, remove and leave to stand for 5 minutes on a cooling rack
- Remove from the mould by gently easing a rounded knife end into the side of the cake; only the top of the cake should be eased from the mould. Pushing the knife too far down could damage your mould and the cake.

Glazing

- Pour the orange juice and honey into a small container and warm in the microwave or on the stove for 2 – 3 seconds
- As it warms, with a pastry brush. mix the honey and juice together.

Tip

Moulds are versatile and can be used for both cooking in the oven and for cold custards or rainbow salads. Moulds can be expensive kitchen items, so they need to be looked after.

The outside of the mould.

The inside of the mould with a lightly oiled underside. It is now ready for the cake mixture.

The golden cooked bundt cake ready to be glazed.

The subtle combination of delicate flavours make this a cake to have any time of the year.

The glazed cake looks mouth-watering as the chosen fruit is added.

The bundt crowned with fresh blueberries. Serve with organic plain yogurt, organic ice cream or organic homemade custard.

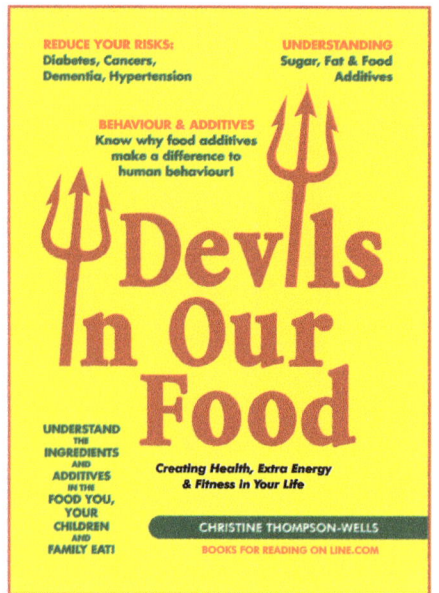

Your Shopping Handbook and App also available at:

www.booksforreadingonline.com

From the Author of

Devils In Our Food

And

Devils In Our Food - Handbook

For just $1.99, please also see the food App at

https://play.google.com/store/apps/details?id=com.hungrels.devilsfood

www.ingramcontent.com/pod-product-compliance
Lightning Source LLC
Chambersburg PA
CBHW061536010526
44107CB00066B/2879